# Willie Wood

## A Bias to
# Bowls

# Willie Wood

## *A Bias to* Bowls

as told to
GORDON DUNWOODIE

Foreword by

DAVID BRYANT, C.B.E.

SPORTSPRINT PUBLISHING

EDINBURGH

ISBN 0 85976 224 6

Phototypeset by Swains, Edinburgh
Printed and bound in Great Britain by Bell & Bain Ltd, Glasgow

# *Foreword*

Bowls is a sport that one can play virtually from the cradle to the grave, and, like most sports, the earlier one takes it up the greater the chance of success, as there is no substitute for a supple body combined with the enthusiasm of youth. William Walker Wood is a prime example, delivering his first bowl at twelve years of age, and the apprenticeship that he served in those most formative years I believe was instrumental in making him one of the finest all-round players in the game.

'Wee Willie', as he is affectionately known to his friends, is equally at home skipping an international four as representing Scotland in a singles event. To me his main strength lies in his adaptability, as over the years he has represented his country with distinction in every position of the game. I well remember his excellent debut for Scotland at lead in 1966, a position he was to fill for several years. It was inevitable, however, that his calm deliberate approach was recognised and he was moved down the order to be groomed for greater things.

As a skip he has been extremely successful at international level and is held in high esteem by his fellow internationals from the four home countries. His shrewd tactical play stems from years of experience, an analytical mind and an intense study of the game he enjoys so much. His popularity as a leader was apparent from the beginning, as his methodical disciplined approach rubs off on his team mates, producing the all-round confidence so necessary for success.

Willie's most recent success was skipping the Scottish four to a 'gold medal' victory in the Commonwealth Games in Auckland N.Z. in 1990. This was an outstanding achievement by any standards, but to those who play the game and have experienced conditions overseas, particularly the faster greens of the southern hemisphere, the performance was even more creditable. The victory in New Zealand will always remain one of the highlights in Willie's life, but as a close friend of this popular Scotsman, I am sure the pinnacle of his bowling career was standing on the dais at the Commonwealth Games, Brisbane in 1982 to receive his gold medal for the Singles event. A single gold medal is always very special, as it is achieved by your efforts alone, but this occasion was more memorable by the way in which it was won. I was fortunate to be present to witness most of the games, and Willie's dominance in the event was complete in as much that against his main rivals he performed at his peak, resulting in convincing wins.

This book relives some of those 'magic moments' and the reader will become involved in the ecstasies of victory and the disappointments of defeat. He will understand the pressures of international sport and realise the years of dedication, discipline, practice and determination required for a bowler to be champion at the highest level.

*David Bryant*

# Contents

# CHAPTER ONE

## *The Early Years*

Fate, that seemingly planned script to destiny, decreed almost inevitably that a fair percentage of my time would be spent on the bowling green.

Gifford, a sleepy East Lothian village of eight hundred inhabitants, didn't offer much in the way of counter attractions to the local bowling club, and having been born into a bowls-mad household it didn't take long before I was trampling the well-worn path to 'the green'.

It's a decision I've never regretted, as the game has, over the years, provided me with an opportunity to travel the world and make friends from every corner of the globe.

The beginnings were by any standards humble.

My father, William Edward Wood, known to all and sundry as 'Camshaft', was manager of Yester Farm, situated just one mile from Gifford.

Both my father and my mother Jennie were born and bred in East Lothian and I followed them into the local Gifford Primary School.

Bowls already played a big part in my father's life, as 'Camshaft' was already a prolific winner, not only in the Gifford Club but in the many open tournaments that abounded in the area at that time.

His other great loves included Heart of Midlothian Football Club, and an enduring passion for motor bikes.

It was the latter that saw him earn his nickname as he was the proud owner of the first motorbike in East Lothian with an overhead camshaft.

The name stuck and over the years the appearance of 'Camshaft' in open tournament draws in the area always assured a big crowd at the green as he was unquestionably one of the game's great characters.

1

My introduction to the game came when I was just twelve years old. Having sneaked the odd 'roll-up' when no-one was around the club, or just before competitions began, I soon realised that in my youthful and modest opinion, I was as good as many of those participating!

After hounding my father and he in turn the local committee members, it was agreed that both William Wood Jnr and one Angus Munro — my schoolmate — would be admitted to membership of the Gifford Bowling Club, but with the proviso that while allowed to play in domestic competitions, entry to the Club Championship would not be permitted until we reached the age of eighteen and attained full membership.

In my case it turned out to have a singularly more lasting effect on my future than on Angus's — he moved out of the area a couple of years later, and I've never seen or heard of him since.

Strangely, when my father was such a keen bowler, it wasn't he who taught me my early lessons in the game. As I recall it, we often argued about the shots to play, and consequently, while remaining very close, we seldom played together.

One of my earliest recollections came during my second season. Having won the Club Handicap Singles in my first year, I was beginning to gather something of a reputation as 'one to keep your eye on', and when I was drawn to play my father in a Singles competition the following year there was a fair bit of interest in the coming battle.

It looked as if I was about to be put firmly in my place when 'Camshaft' opened up a 20-10 lead, but as I was to learn, time without number, that last shot can invariably prove the most difficult to get and I came back to win 21-20.

Any thoughts though of self-appraisal were quickly dispelled when my father informed me that 'O.K. you've won today but you'll lose your next round match in the competition', and he was proved correct as the bubble burst in no uncertain terms.

A big influence on my career at that time was Gifford member Colin Campbell, an Edinburgh butcher who had retired to

*My brief football career with the Gifford Youth Team
(bottom left) at the tender age of just twelve.*

Gifford and spent much of his leisure time at the bowling green.

Mr Campbell for some reason obviously took a shine to young Willie Wood, and offered me the princely sum of half-a-crown every time I won a tie. It was just the boost I needed and I picked up quite a bit in the way of pocket money from my beneficiary who stuck to his word over the years and never once missed out on my 'reward'.

In future years, when I was omitted from the 1986 Commonwealth Games side for not measuring up to the strict interpretation of the amateur status as defined by the Commonwealth Games Officials, I couldn't help recalling those half-crown payouts at Gifford and wondering whether, had they been public knowledge, I would have been out of the 1974, '78 and '82 Games!

But while bowls was beginning to take up more and more of my time there were still the visits to Tynecastle Park to see Hearts in action and further satisfy the sporting appetite.

The fortnightly visits to every Hearts home match were a long-established family tradition. I myself had stopped playing football when just twelve years of age, principally because of my growing love affair with bowls, but my passion for the 'Jam Tarts' was as strong as ever.

Indeed, my full name — William Walker Wood — comes from the legendary Tommy Walker who played for Hearts in the pre-war days and went on to manage the Club throughout the 1950s.

These Tynecastle visits came as a welcome break from the rigours of a Scottish winter. With Indoor Bowls still very much in its infancy, opportunities for bowlers in the winter months were still very limited and the chance to turn to the country's national sport was much welcomed.

And the journeys back to Gifford were a major part of it, as the game was replayed through different eyes, players' performances analysed, and expert advice offered on the team selection for the next week's encounter.

My early teenage years seemed to be spent between Tynecastle and Gifford Bowling Club, and while still barred from competing in the Club Singles Championship I had found myself playing in the local league when aged just fourteen.

But the wait to play in the Club Championship proved well worthwhile when I took the title at my first attempt — just a few months after my eighteenth birthday — and that same season I made my debut in the East Lothian Scottish Counties Championship side.

However, with my bowls career just beginning to take off, it had all to be put on ice for the next three years when I was called up for National Service.

I opted for the Army and signed on for an extra third year with the Royal Electrical Mechanical Engineers — R.E.M.E. — and spent the vast majority of my time in Germany.

Unlike many of my contemporaries I can look back and truthfully say I enjoyed my spell in the Services — it taught me among other things discipline and independence — something that has stood me in good stead ever since.

I returned from the Army in 1959, but too late to play bowls with the season having ended the previous month, and it was the following year before I got back on the green. East Lothian,

*Colin Campbell, my first sponsor.*

despite having won the Hamilton Trophy in 1957 — my first year in the Army — still found a place for me in their side, and just two years later I played my first International Trial Match.

The match was played at the Northern Club and despite a reasonable performance I didn't manage to catch the selectors' eye although a man who was to become a good friend and rival over the years — Newbattle's Alec McIntosh — won his first international honours.

But my lifestyle was quickly taking shape. The family had moved from the farm two years earlier into Gifford itself and I had been working as a mechanic in the local garage since returning from the Army with my spare time spent increasingly at the bowling green.

Bowls had always played an important part in my life and it was continuing to do so. Realising that I had a fair degree of ability I was determined to put as much time and effort into the game and see just how much of a name I could make for myself in it.

I found this no great hardship as I've always had a tremendous appetite for the game and enjoy all aspects of it. I love being involved in it, and when not playing there's nothing better than the after-match post mortem on how you won or what went wrong. I enjoy spectating too but above all I love to play the game and I'm sure that has been a big factor in my success — you only get out of any sport what you put into it and while I contribute a lot in terms of time and effort I enjoy every minute of it.

The International Trial too had whetted my appetite for top-class competition. I am by nature a competitive person and I like to play to win. That is not to say that you don't accept defeat when it comes along. Bowls, by its very nature, has more imponderables in it than any other sport.

I cannot offhand think of any other game where you can play four perfect shots and have them taken off you by your opponent with not necessarily a good shot.

There is a larger degree of luck, or, as bowlers put it, 'rubs of the green' than in any other sport — and in saying that I don't want to minimise the skill factor in the game.

In snooker, for example, when you are at the table and scoring your opponent can only sit and watch. In darts when you are throwing, your opponent cannot influence your performance. But in bowls often there is no reward on an end for four perfectly played bowls as your opponent has sneaked one in and your bowls consequently count for nothing.

That having been said, often it is a case of making your own luck by keeping your opponent constantly under pressure. That is why over a period of time the good player will come out on top, but part of the attraction, indeed fascination of bowls, is that on just the odd occasion the underdog can upset the odds.

I believe that is one of the main reasons why the game has remained free from the tantrums and fits of temper so often displayed by leading exponents of other sports.

In bowls, you play hard — very hard — but you are aware that if it's your opponent's day then there is not a lot you can do about it. Your turn will come, and while you battle till the last bowl, if you lose — you lose. There's always tomorrow!

That's an attitude I developed at an early stage of my bowls career and I have seen no reason to change my opinion since then.

My disappointment at not making the international side in 1962 was tempered somewhat as Hearts lifted the First Division Championship for the second time in three years but, undaunted, I resolved to make an international cap an early priority.

Whether I was ready to take a place in the Scottish side at that time is debatable. I was after all only twenty-four years of age, and while many players are now seasoned campaigners at that age it was different back in 1962. I was still very much a youngster in an old man's game, and on reflection I think the four-year wait until my first cap in 1966 did me no harm at all.

The following year saw the family dealt a devastating blow and suddenly bowls did not seem so important after all.

My younger brother Ronald, seven years my junior at seventeen years old, died in a tragic accident. Whilst visiting my grandmother, Ronald and two schoolfriends set off from her house in the direction of a local pond not far from Yester Farm, and boys being boys, the three set out on the pond in a hastily constructed "raft". The inevitable happened, the raft sank and while his two friends survived, Ronald drowned.

It took weeks before anyone in the family could come to terms with what had happened and Ronald's death seemed to dominate our thoughts and actions for a long, long time. But slowly, the realisation that life had to go on was accepted and all in the family tried to restructure their lives with the realisation that Ronald would no longer be part of it.

# CHAPTER TWO

## *Coming to the Fore*

Slowly after Ronald's death I began to get back to the bowling green, but despite retaining my place in the East Lothian Hamilton Trophy side, there was no international trial in 1963 or for that matter in either of the two following years.

But my breakthrough came in 1965 when I teamed up with one of the best bowlers Edinburgh ever produced — Balerno's Jackie Forrest. It really was a perfect example of youth and experience, with yours truly now twenty-seven and Jackie a few days short of his sixty-fourth birthday when we set out on the trail of the Edinburgh Open Pairs Tournament Title.

I had come close in the Edinburgh Tournament back in 1961, when Jack Christie from the Northern Club just edged me out 21-19 in the singles final, but this time Jackie and I were destined to win.

The final fell on Jackie's birthday — an omen if ever there was one — and we eventually ran out comfortable 17-8 winners against Pilrig's Jim Paterson and Andrew Watson from Maitland.

We opened with doubles on the first two ends but back came Jim and Andrew with two singles and a three to lead 5-4 after five ends. The next four ends could hardly have been tighter with Jackie and I scoring two singles, losing one, and the eighth end a 'no' shot, to leave things nicely balanced at 6-6 after nine ends. Then the game took a big swing in our favour. We scored three shots on the next end followed by a single before we dropped a single on the twelfth end, but doubles on the next two put us well in command at 14-7 with just three ends to play.

Andrew and Jim hit back with a single on the fifteenth end but when we picked up a three on the penultimate end we were

8

out of sight at 17-8 and the title was ours without playing the last end.

Little did I know then, but that was to be the beginning of a great spell in the Edinburgh Tournament, not only for myself, but for the family and the Gifford Club.

Towards the end of 1965, I was approached by Scottish Bowling Association Councillor Willie Dick who explained the intricacies of selection in the international side.

There existed at that time a system of "nomination" before a player could be chosen for an international trial.

Basically only players in their County's Hamilton Trophy side were considered for selection, but in addition the international hopeful had to be nominated by his club, as, in their opinion, worthy of a trial.

Willie Dick pointed out to me that Gifford had not been nominating me and suggested I brought the matter up with the Club; that I duly did and received the nomination for the 1966 season.

That was of course no guarantee that it would bring a trial, but fortunately East Lothian had a fairly good season in the Hamilton Trophy, going all the way to the final before losing out to Ayrshire, and when the trial side was announced I was named at lead in a rink skipped by Dick Bernard.

The trial was held at the Willowbrae Club and we played against a rink skipped by probably the greatest character ever produced in Scots bowls circles — Harry Reston, who at that time played out of the Seafield Club in Bathgate.

Harry had been an ever-present in the Scots side between 1957 and 1961 but he had missed out in the side in 1962 and had been out since. The ebullient Harry was desperate to get back into the side and we enjoyed a real 'ding-dong' battle before we finally won by four shots.

I was pleased with my game and more so when Harry told me that he thought I had a good chance of making the side.

On the debit side was the fact that Scotland had won the previous year's championship in London — only their second win in twelve years — and it was widely expected there would not be many changes in the side.

That was the way it worked out, with fifteen of the side retaining their places but of the other five — three new caps and two recalls — the name of W.W. Wood (Gifford) was listed.

I well remember hearing the news. I had been playing at Tanfield in the club's annual charity tournament and was just about to leave the green when the news reached the club that I had been named in the Scottish side. My first reaction was one of whether there could have been a mistake, then when it began to sink in, one of mild fear!

Was I really good enough to compete at that level? What if it all went wrong and I froze when the action began? But quickly I began to come to terms with it and equally that those who had picked me obviously reckoned that I was good enough . . . and if they thought that, who was I to argue with them!

The other new caps in the side were the then current Scottish Champion, John Hershaw, and Willie Dyet, and Harry Reston recalled along with Bob Motroni.

Dick Bernard, who had skipped my rink in the trial, was named as reserve — his first international honour — as was another man who was to have a long and distinguished career with Scotland — Rennie Logan from Kirkliston.

The full side named for the series at Queen's Park, Glasgow, between the 6th and 8th of July was:

RINK 1          W. Smith (Galston L.W.M.) L. Brown (Forfar)
                W. Adrain (Dreghorn) and W. Moore (Dreghorn)
                Skip

RINK 2          J. Christie (Edinburgh Northern) R. D. Adamson
                (Carluke) S. Grant (Mauchline) and C. Craig
                (Queen's Park) Skip

RINK 3          J. Hershaw (Ardeer Recreation) J. Devlin
                (Auchinleck) J. McRae (Coatdyke) and J. McAtee
                (Catrine) Skip

RINK 4          W.W. Wood (Gifford) R. Thomson (Deans)
                R. Motroni (Dumfries) and J. Hamilton
                (Hamilton) Skip

RINK 5          A.G. Blair (Rosyth) W. Irvine (Alva)
                W. Dyet (Balerno) and H. Reston (Seafield) Skip

RESERVES   A.R. Logan (Kirkliston) and R. Bernard
                (Gorebridge)

*Jackie Forrest and me after our Edinburgh Open Pairs win in 1975.*

Jimmy Hamilton was also named as Captain of the side, and looking back on it, I couldn't have wished for a better rink in which to have made my international debut. It was a memorable experience — one that will stay with me all of my life, and what a way to launch your international career — Scotland retained their title, and on a personal basis my rink won all three of their matches. Indeed three of the Scottish rinks won all three matches — our own, Harry Reston's and Willie Moore's.

Scotland started with a 23-shot win over Ireland on the opening day, added a 39-shot win over Wales, and then went to town on the last day, romping to a record 56-shot win over England, with all five rinks finishing on the credit side.

And, by all accounts, yours truly had a saisfactory début. Gordon Duncan, in the *News of the World,* wrote:

> Most impressive of the three newcomers was 28 year old Willie Wood of Gifford, whose leading for Hamilton was first class.

So my international career, which is dealt with in greater detail elsewhere in this book, was off and running.

But, back in 1966, international bowls meant the three-day Home International Series. There were none of the invitation events that pack the calendar nowadays and, after the Queen's Park action it was back to the local tournament scene . . . and the Edinburgh Open Tournament was due to start the following week.

Jackie Forrest and I were again in the pairs line-up, defending the title we won the previous year, and we were both in the singles line-up. In situations like that bowlers always have the understanding that if the two events should clash, then the singles should take precedence — rather like tennis players do at Wimbledon where it's not unusual to see a double partnership scratch as one or other of them is going well in the singles.

And, as luck would have it, that was how we lost our pairs title. After a couple of early wins, we survived a fightback to score a 14-13, third-round win over Sighthill's J. Steele and T. McMorran, but not long after that we had to scratch as I had made it through to the semi-final of the singles.

My semi-final opponent was a real seasoned campaigner — Frank Henderson from the Whitehouse and Grange Club — and what a battle I had before edging home 21-19. With both Frank and I playing well the big crowd at Balgreen thoroughly enjoyed a great tactical battle.

I had the best of the early exchanges and when I counted on five successive ends the scoreboard showed me with a handy 14-7 lead. Slowly Frank began to eat into my lead, and after 23 ends he was right back in it trailing by just one shot at 19-20, but in a real cliffhanger of a finish, I managed to snatch the shot I needed to book my final place.

My opponent was 48-year-old Alex Ross from Balerno. Alex, a past Balerno champion, had played in his club rink that had won the Scottish Fours Championship two years earlier and was by any standards a formidable adversary. Like me, Alex had survived a tense semi-final battle before he too carded a 21-19 win over Ayr's John Ross.

But my hopes of adding the single title to last season's

pairs win soon ended when I went down 17-21 to Alex, who turned in a sparkling display. He opened with a single on the first end but I managed to pick up the jack with my third delivery on the next end and I then drew another shot with my last bowl to lead 2-1. Undaunted, Alex hit back with two successive doubles to lead 5-2 before I counted a three on the fifth end to tie things at five-all.

On the next end, I ditched the jack to pick up a single and edge into the lead again at 6-5 before Alex hit back with a count of three to lead 8-6, and he maintained that advantage throughout most of the match, finally winning 21-17 and leaving me thwarted for the second time in my ambition of an Edinburgh Open Singles win.

But I didn't have to wait much longer for my singles win, making it third time lucky the following year — and what a real family affair finals day turned out to be.

As in the previous year, the Tournament followed on immediately after the international series — hosted this time by Wales — and Scotland won all three matches to retain the championship and complete a hat-trick of wins.

Back in Edinburgh, I again made it through to the final of the singles after a 21-10 semi-final victory over Bob Thom of Bainfield. I found myself just having the better of the early exchanges and led 12-10 after fourteen ends, but then I hit a purple patch and a burst of 1, 3, 3 and 2 saw me safely through to the final again.

It looked odds on that I would face one of my international colleagues in the final — or so the pundits thought. The other last four battle brought together Willie Dyet, who had made his international debut with me at Queen's Park the previous year, and a man whose form I knew well — my 21-year-old cousin Brian Bissett who three years earlier had taken my record as the youngest ever championship winner at Gifford — winning it like me at eighteen years of age but taking the record by a few months.

Twice during the early exchanges Willie counted a maximum four — the second time to put him into the lead at 13-12 after fourteen ends. But undaunted, Brian hit back and picked up eight shots for the loss of just two over the next eight ends to lead 20-15.

Back came Willie again and two singles and a double took his total to 19 before Brian finally clinched a 21-19 win with a single on the twenty-sixth end.

So my final opponent this time would be my cousin, and just to continue the family theme, my father won through to the pairs final in partnership with my semi-final victim from last year — Frank Henderson. They went through to the final with a 14-10 win over Dalkeith pair Willie Gardiner and Ronnie Harris and lined up against Ormiston pair Peter and Alec Ballantyne, who came through 14-6 against Jimmy Ferguson and Charlie Kinnear of Craigentinny.

For a long time it looked as if my singles jinx was about to strike again. Brian was quickly into his stride and led 3-0 after two ends. I opened my account with singles on the third and fourth ends. Back came Brian to extend his lead to 7-3 after eight ends and then a maximum count of four on the ninth end saw Brian suddenly well in command at 11-3.

It looked as if I would need to settle for second place again, when Brian maintained his advange to lead 17-9, but then I began to find my touch and, helped by two counts of three and two badly played strikes from Brian, I edged into an 18-17 lead after twenty-two ends.

A single on the next increased my advantage, and with me lying shot on the next end Brian turned one of my bowls into the head to give me the two shots I needed for a 21-17 win.

I felt sorry for Brian, particularly as he had held such a commanding lead, but it's all part of the game and I know it did him no harm in his bowls education and he went on to win an indoor international cap in 1983.

The icing was added to the cake when my father took the pairs title with a 20-16 win, and how the Gifford Club celebrated that night well into the 'wee sma' oors', but if we thought that was really something, we had no idea that within a matter of weeks we would be celebrating Gifford's first-ever Scottish Championship win.

CHAPTER THREE

# Like Father Like Son . . . Almost

I hardly had time to savour my first Edinburgh Open Singles win than I was back in the thick of the action again . . . and at the same Balgreen venue. The Champion of Champions Tournament, as the name suggests, brings together the current champions of the tournaments in the Edinburgh area.

My semi-final opponent was John Scott from the Ardmillan Club who was later to notch up eighteen indoor international appearances for Scotland, and John made a great start, scoring on three of the first four ends to lead 5-1. Six ends later the gap was still the same with John 9-5 ahead and playing well.

Two ends later John's advantage had grown to five shots at 11-6 but I managed to pick up three shots on the next end, the thirteenth, and a double on the following end tied things up at 11-11. John edged ahead again 16-13 after eighteen ends but, changing the jack to full length, allowed me to find my touch and I went on to win 21-18.

That put me through to a place in the evening final against Craigentinny's George Aitken who had come through 21-16 in his semi-final against Dave McDonald, a seasoned campaigner from Ormiston.

The final, for a change, saw me make a good start, opening up a 7-0 lead before George opened his account, but I maintained my advantage and after seventeen ends I was within sight of victory at 18-9. George then enjoyed his best end, picking up a maximum count of four, but a double and single on the nineteenth and twentieth ends saw me safely through to a 21-13 win.

Life was beginning to take on a busy pace, and with the local press full of my two triumphs they were beginning to predict great things for me. But it was another member of the family who was destined to make the headlines over the next few weeks.

Plans were well afoot for me to tie the matrimonial knot, having become engaged the previous year. The subject of my attention was Morag Turnbull who had begun to frequent the local haunts in Gifford and the surrounding areas some five years earlier. Morag's parents had a summer house not far from the village, and her attendance at the local dances and social functions over the years had led to a romance that had seen us decide to take the plunge. Almost inevitably however our wedding plans, while not entirely upset by the bowls calendar, were to some extent overshadowed by the events of the previous weekend.

For bowls enthusiasts the first Friday and Saturday in August traditionally means the annual pilgrimage to Glasgow for the final stages of the National Championships. It really is the highlight of the season with anything up to four thousand spectators cramming into the grounds of the Queen's Park Club to cast their expert eye over the proceedings.

And as well as the action, there's the off-green activities where more than just a few tipples are enjoyed as old friendships are cemented and new ones forged in the clubhouse or bar-tent.

This year, however, there was more than just the usual interest as my father had won through to the last sixteen stage in the singles. It was his sixth time through to the final stages and the third time he had qualified in the singles, but until then Gifford were still looking for a first 'Scottish' triumph.

The omens were good, however. I am a great believer that in bowls when you are on the crest of a wave, then things go well for you and there is no doubt that the summer of 1967 was, by any standards, quite a time for the Wood family. It was with more than the usual degree of optimism that we set out for Queen's Park where 'Camshaft' was due to open his title bid against John Jardine of Dundonald.

The first game on the Friday morning is invariably a bit of a scramble with the sixteen-strong field reduced to half in one fell swoop. In these circumstances, it is all about surviving, and

*1967 . . . and "Camshaft" returns to Gifford with the Scottish Singles Championship*

'Camshaft' did just that, winning 21-12 to move through to a quarter-final date with a man who was already figuring increasingly in my bowls life — and would to a greater degree over the next few years — Gorebridge's Dick Bernard.

It was a real ding-dong affair but a 21-15 win put father through to a semi-final shot the following morning against Inverkeithing's Peter Coleman.

Coleman, at twenty-seven years of age, was turning into the surprise packet of the championship and what a tremendous battle ensued. The young Fifer scored on the first three ends to lead 6-0 but slowly 'Camshaft' began to haul himself into the battle and with seven ends played he had reduced the deficit to just two shots at 5-7. The next end then provided the turning point with Peter playing a bad running shot that removed his own bowl followed by a badly grassed, tight delivery with his final bowl, allowing my father to pick up a maximum count of four and edge ahead for the first time at 9-7.

From that point on 'Camshaft' was always in command and he quickly raced to within one shot of victory at 20-12. But, as so often happens, that last shot turned out to be the hardest one of them all to get. Slowly Coleman hauled himself back into contention as he took his total to 17 before disaster struck.

Another attempt at a running bowl saw him repeat his folly of the eighth end and he again took out his own shot bowl to leave a relieved Gifford man the 21-17 winner. His final opponent was Camelon's Jimmy Amos, who at fifty-nine was two years his junior. Amos, in his first appearance at Queen's Park, had clinched his final spot with a 21-14 win over Lanarkshire's big hope for the title, John Hunter of Houldsworth.

By contrast to the brilliant form showed by both players in their morning semi-final, the early exchanges were scrappy. But father opened with a double on the first end and three more on the next saw him open up a handy 5-0 lead. Amos opened his account with a single on the next end but that was the only bright spell in the early exchanges for the Camelon man, and a run of 1, 1, 3 and 1 saw 'Camshaft' into an 11-1 lead. From that point on, there was only going to be one winner and although Jimmy Amos fought to the last, father coasted to a comfortable 21-8 win.

His delight was obvious, and his comments after his win will stay with me always: 'If I never win anything again, I won't mind — I have now achieved my greatest ambition', he told wellwishers seconds after his victory, but then the competitive spirit rekindled itself, and he added: 'Mind you, I'm not saying I won't be doing my best in the British Championship next month.'

Sadly, his best wasn't good enough, losing out 21-15 to English Champion Bill Irish in the semi-final at the Belmont Club in Belfast, but 'Camshaft' had achieved his life's ambition with his Scottish Singles victory and as he himself said — anything else was a bonus.

The scenes in the Gifford Club after father's win were really something. When we arrived back in Gifford a piper met the car carrying my father and he was hauled shoulder-high by wellwishers who paraded him through the village to the bowling green, preceded by the piper, with 'Camshaft' proudly holding the Rosebery Trophy aloft for all to see.

The clubhouse had been hastily decorated and celebrations went on well into the morning. Indeed the revelry reached such a pitch that the new Scottish Champion had to leave off bowling for a couple of days after straining his back during the knees-up.

With all the excitement, my wedding date had slipped round almost unnoticed, but the following Saturday Morag and I made it to Kirkgate Church in Leith where we were duly married. We set up home in Haddington where we stayed for a couple of years before moving the four miles back to Gifford.

Father's win in the Scottish singles strengthened my ambition to win the title. A Scottish Singles win is the ambition of every bowler, and I am no exception, but to follow on and win the title your father has won before you must be something special. I thought I might just do that the following season. I had a great run in the National Singles and went right through to win my S.B.A. District title. That put me one game away from Queen's Park, and standing between me and that August date was Willie White from Spittal, but I ran into a man in inspired form, and Willie beat me 21-19. His run however ended at the quarter-final stage when he crashed to a 21-5 defeat against eventual winner Jock Lamont of Kirn.

But my chance to emulate my father's 'Scottish' win came two years later when I made it through to Queen's Park in the singles.

In retrospect, I suppose I could have picked an easier year for my title bid, as, looking back on it now, there were more than just a few useful players through to the final stages that year. As well as myself, two others had gained international honours — Dick Bernard and Roy White from Goldenacre — and George Downie Jnr (Strathaven), Willie Nimmo (Slamannan) and Davie McPherson (Dunfermline Northern) were all destined to make the international arena later in their careers.

My first opponent was Jim Reid from the Barrowfield Club and I had a comfortable 21-11 win and followed that up with a 21-15 win over Brechin's Willie Reid to put me through to the semi-final, where I played Hill Waddell from Meikleriggs. Waddell was very much the outsider in the eyes of the pundits but he played very well and I had to be at my best to survive. I made a good start and led 5-0 after three ends but back came Waddell with a burst of 1, 1, 2 and 3 to take the lead at 7-5.

After twelve ends things could have not been more evenly balanced with the scores locked together at 9-9, and then it was my turn to enjoy a run of 1, 2 and 1, to put me 13-9 ahead. The next few ends were nip and tuck with the decisive point a three that I picked up on the eighteenth end, helping me into a 20-14 lead, and I clinched the winning single when a measure to a ditched jack on the twenty-third end gave me a 21-14 win.

I didn't have to wait long to find out my final opponent as Dick Bernard came through his semi-final with Roy White to set up the first-ever all East of Scotland final. Bernard beat White 21-11.

So just three years after my father's Scottish Singles win I was within one match of taking the title back to Gifford, fulfilling my life's ambition, and completing the first-ever father and son double in the championship.

The early exchanges were tight but with four ends played I found myself trailing 4-2. Dick then produced four perfect deliveries on the next end to score a maximum four, and a single on the sixth put me deep in bother, trailing 2-9. My hopes were briefly raised when I turned Dick's nearest bowl through the head to count three on the next end, but Dick hit back immediately with another maximum to lead 13-5 and really my last chance had gone.

Dick, firing on all cylinders, went on to win 21-8, to leave me a very dispirited player. In retrospect I think I met the best single-handed bowler in Scotland at that particular time. I reckon against anyone else I would have had more than an even chance of taking the title, but at that point Dick Bernard was quite simply in a class by himself and it was just my bad luck to run into him in full flow.

So that was the immediate end to my hopes of emulating my father's win in the Scottish Singles, and in the intervening years I've never been as close again.

However it still remains my major ambition, and it was a disappointing note to end the 1970 season on. Meanwhile Morag and I had settled back into Gifford and our daughter Sylvia, born on 30th May 1968, was now two years old and taking up more of our time.

# CHAPTER FOUR

## *The World Awaits . . . South Africa*

After the 1970 season, things were relatively quiet for a couple of years. Scotland's international side continued to carry all before them in the Home International Championship but, with the exception of the Commonwelath Games and the World Championships, there were virtually no opportunities to test your form against the overseas countries, and with both these events held at four-year intervals, there was a distinct lack of international competition.

But that was to change when towards the end of the 1972 season a letter dropped through the letterbox at 26 Walden Terrace telling me that I had been chosen by the Selection Committee of the Scottish Bowling Association to represent Scotland in the South African Open International Games in Pretoria the following March-April.

The fourteen-day event was split between a pairs and singles championship with no less than seventeen countries participating. I couldn't help but have a quiet chuckle to myself when I noted from the letter that my partner would be none other than that man Bernard again, but this time I was more than happy to see Dick's name listed next to mine. While I knew he would provide stern opposition when the singles began, I couldn't have wished for a better pairs partner, and on my first trip overseas I knew Dick and I would be more than compatible off the green too.

The five-month wait from the official notification to actually leaving for South Africa seemed an eternity, but the birth of our son Colin, the previous April, did help to take my mind off the impending trip. However, it also proved time to contemplate what was ahead, and it was with a strange mixture of fear and expectation that I planned my campaign against the world's top bowlers.

22

*If you want to get ahead . . . get a hat. South Africa Games 1973*

The fear came in realising that you were going in on your own against the top names in the game. The rink format used in the Home Internationals hardly prepared you for top-class singles play, and while I enjoy singles best of all, there was that niggling doubt. . . . could I compete at that level against players of that calibre? Another worry was the venue — South Africa. What would playing conditions be like? . . . . Could I adjust to the faster greens? . . . . the imponderables seemed endless.

I've often wondered whether Dick shared these thoughts on the build-up to South Africa. It's something I've never really discussed with him, but knowing him as I think I do, I'm sure he had a few little worries as well. By comparison with the present day's big money events, where even first-round losers are picking up four-figure cheques, it's interesting to note that not only was no payment involved, but no allowance was made for loss of wages.

That is one aspect of life in which I have been very lucky. I was a married man with two small children and it would have been very easy for Morag to be less than enthusiastic about my participation in bowls and the increasing demands the game was making on both my time and finances, but I can honestly say that from the outset, she has backed me one hundred per cent in everything. On the other side of the coin, as a humble mechanic from a little Scots village, I've been given the opportunity to see places and countries that, under normal circumstances, could have been little more than a dream.

The Scottish Bowling Association supplied Dick and myself with the usual blazer, white trousers, cardigan, tie and hat. A hat! That was to be a new experience playing bowls in the 'panama': that's mandatory in countries like South Africa, where the seering overhead sun can take its toll on the unsuspecting.

Eventually our departure day arrived and the first part of it was to provide Dick and me with the first of many new experiences. Neither of us had flown before and I well remember Morag's comment as we sat in the airport waiting for our flight to be called. 'I bet the two of you would be quite happy if the whole thing was called off right now and you headed back home', she quipped, and I can tell you there was more than just a grain of truth in it.

However, the flight was called and after emotional goodbyes we were on our way. South Africa had already been named to host the 1976 World Championships, and while there were many sports involved in the '73 Games, the bowls events took on added importance as a 'dry run' for the World Championships three years later. On arrival in Pretoria, we were transferred to the Pretoria Burgers Hotel, our home for the next two weeks, and the first thing that struck us was how tight the security was.

Immediately we entered the Hotel, we were photographed for our official passes and were instructed to wear them at all times. On one particular occasion Dick and I left our room to go downstairs to the hotel foyer, leaving our identity cards in our room. What a fracas! Two security guards spotted us, and

*Edmonton Commonwealth Games 1978*

after a few questions we were marched to our rooms to prove who we were.

The two guards left after we gave them some of our S.B.A. badges — normally reserved for exchanging with your opponents — but on this occasion, discretion proved to be the better part of valour and what could have been an unfortunate inci-

25

dent finished with much laughter, handshakes all round, and as a parting shot a polite but firm reminder that 'Identity Cards must be worn at all times Meester Wood and Bernard'.

The scene of the action was the Berea Park Club which boasted three magnificent greens and a clubhouse that was by any standards sumptuous. The pairs competition was the first of the two events and we started well, beating Malawi 23-11, before drawing 21 all with Australia and then adding wins over Jersey (33-13), and Guernsey (25-12).

We lost our first game when home country pair Tom Harvey and Doug Watson beat us 24-16, and then we figured in our second share of the spoils, drawing 19-19 with England's Peter Line and David Bryant, before losing out again, this time going down 20-24 to Rhodesia. We halted the slide, beating Wales 24-14, but then went down 16-18 to Israel. My first experience of a truly international field was beginning to be something of a baptism of fire, but thankfully we got back on the rails and finished with four successive wins in the round-robin event.

The run started with a 25-14 win over Ireland, followed by a 25-9 victory over Hong Kong, and a 21-10 triumph over Canada, and finished with a hard-fought 21-18 success over the United States. That left us out of the medals, but a record of eight wins, three defeats, and two draws left us reasonably happy with our display and set us up nicely for the singles battles to come.

The amazing things about the South African greens was how they stood up to the rigours of a hard competition — indeed they improved as the events progressed. That is indicative of the standard of greens throughout the country — they really have got their priorities correct and the on-green activities are always the first and foremost priority in their consideration.

When the singles began, I met Dick Folkins of the United States in my opening match and I was happy to kick-off with a 21-10 win. While that was pleasing, it was nothing compared with my second match against George 'Saco' Delgado of Hong Kong. I had seen Delgado three years earlier in Edinburgh when he was a member of the Colonies rink that took the gold

*On my way to the Gold Medal at the South African Games in 1973*

medal at the Commonwealth Games and he looked a more than useful player.

It turned out to be just one of those games, however, with everything I tried coming off and everything George tried going wrong, and it was all over in just twelve ends with George failing to score and a slightly embarrassed Willie Wood slipping into the clubhouse a 21-0 winner. But bowls has a way of bouncing back and flattening you just when you least expect it, and in my very next match, Australia's Barry Salter brought me back to earth with a very firm bump, winning 21-16.

That was hardly the confidence booster I wanted before my next match against the man the locals were tipping to take the title — their own Tommy Harvey. I had never seen Harvey play but his reputation preceded him and I knew I would need to be at my best to survive. It turned into a real ding-dong battle but in the end I got home 21-17, and suddenly a few people in South Africa were beginning to sit up and take notice — and just a few were asking if it was possible that 'Wee Willie' could go all the way and win the event.

My next opponent was a man I knew well from my sojourns with Scotland in the Home International Championships — England's Peter Line, and a 21-13 win saw my title challenge begin to gather momentum. There followed two comfortable wins, a 21-11 triumph over Roy du-Feu of Guernsey and a 21-9 victory against Israel's Matt Gordon, but my next game, the eighth-round match against Ellis Stanbury of Wales, saw a real nail-biter before I scraped home 21-20.

I stretched my winning run with a 21-9 win over Malawi's Harry Lakin and then found myself down to meet another man who had a big reputation — Bill Jackson from Rhodesia. We were scheduled to play in the afternoon but at the appointed time there was no sign of my opponent. Eventually, an embarrassed Bill arrived at the green well after the half-hour grace allowed by the laws of the game and explained that in attempting to enjoy some rest before the game, he had fallen asleep and missed the scheduled starting time.

The officials ruled that the match would be awarded to me if I didn't wish to play now that Bill had arrived, but really there was no choice for me to make. I told them that I had come to South Africa to play bowls, not to win matches in committee rooms and on technicalities and that I was ready to play whenever Bill was. It was a decision that I am sure won me a few friends, but really if you attempt to use situations like that to win games, at the end of the day you are only cheating yourself, and I would like to think that if a similar situation arose in reverse, my opponent would give me the benefit of the doubt.

It all worked out quite well anyway with Bill more upset over the incident than I was and I went on to score a comfortable 21-9 win. That gave me nine wins from ten matches and, with just three games to play, a place in the final was now very much in my thoughts. It came a step nearer with a 21-11 win over Billy Pimley from Ireland, and a 21-6 victory over Canada's Bruce Matheson saw me just one game away from a final place.

My opponent was one of the old stagers of the international circuit — Jersey's Joe Dolan — but I got off to a good start, had Joe under pressure from an early stage and went through to the final with a 21-8 win.

My opponent was none other than the great man himself — David John Bryant — who had also qualified from his group with twelve wins from his thirteen matches — his only defeat coming at the hands of Rhodesia's Ian MacMillan. Strangely, while I had played against David Bryant in various games, that was our first meeting in singles play and it was to be the start of an intense rivalry and friendship that was to continue over the ensuing years.

The final was played the day after Colin's first birthday, and while I was disappointed not to be at home to enjoy the special family occasion, I reckoned the best birthday present I could bring my son back from South Africa would be a gold medal. I've always enjoyed playing in South Africa — I like the people and they are very knowledgeable where bowls are concerned, and they certainly turned out in droves for the final.

Official figures weren't available but one local newpspaper stated that 8,000 people turned out to watch the final, and while I think they let their enthusiasm take over in estimating the attendance, there were certainly a good few thousand packed in the stands round the four sides of the green.

As one would expect in a final of that importance, the early exchanges were tentative, with little between David and myself. David just got the better of things to lead 7-5 after eight ends, but then I began to find my drawing weight with greater consistency and five ends later I had moved in front at 13-8. We traded doubles on the next two ends before my big break came on the sixteenth end. I was lying two shots when David elected to strike, but he was off target, took his own bowl out to give me a full count of four and suddenly I was 19-10 ahead and within two of victory.

Back came David with a single on the next end but I tied it all

*Note the sartorial
elegance . . . at the
Skol Awards Dinner
in 1974*

up when two shots on the eighteenth end gave me a 21-11 victory and the title. It was a moment that would stay with me forever. Here I was, on the other side of the world, taking on and
beating the world's top players — and what better way to win
any event than to beat the current World and Commonwealth
Champion in the final. My only regret was that none of my family could be there to share the great moment with me.

My win created quite a stir, and when I returned home there
was a crowd of wellwishers on hand to add their good wishes,
and over the next few weeks letters of congratulations poured
into my home in Gifford.

There were letters from family friends, East Lothian Bowling Association, all the clubs in the surrounding area, and one
from the Scottish Bowling Association — which brought me
back to earth, as it also contained something of a rap on the
knuckles!

The letter, signed by Secretary Alex Provan read:

Dear Willie,

The President, Office Bearers, and Members of the Council wish to convey sincere congratulations to you on your outstanding performance in the recent South African Games. To have won the Gold Medal in the Singles by overcoming such renowned opposition is an achievement of which we and all bowlers are very proud and we feel particularly happy in the knowledge that our selection has been so fully justified. Our thanks go to you for so admirably hoisting the flag of Scotland in the field of World Bowls.

We realise you will have had much to occupy your attention but are somewhat disappointed that the only official confirmation we have received about the Games and results in both Competitions has been the newspaper announcement of your victory in the Singles. You may recall that in my letter of 16th March, I asked if you would bring copies of the Official brochure with a record of all the scores and also our National Flag. If you can submit these items now I shall be grateful.

Yours sincerely

ALEX PROVAN
Secretary

Paperwork never was one of my favourite pastimes, and the brochures and flag were hastily despatched to 50 Wellington Street, Glasgow. Having just given my international standing a major boost, the last thing I wanted was to fall foul of the powers that be.

# CHAPTER FIVE

## Commonwealth Games . . . Bronze in '74, Silver in '78

My win in the '73 South African Games saw me widely tipped for the Commonwealth Games side the following year, and the feeling was that I would also be back in South Africa in 1976 for the World Championships.

I felt myself, that provided I had a good solid 1973 season, I would be in the Commonwealth Games side. As for 1976, well, that was a long way off and the immediate plan was to secure a place in the squad for Christchurch the following year. The season turned out well, particularly the international series at Bournemouth where I was named as Scottish Team Captain. It's always a great honour to represent your country, but being named as captain added the icing to the cake, and with Scotland going for their ninth successive win my delight was also tinged with a little worry as I didn't want to be captain when the run came to an end. My fears however were groundless.

I was again chosen as lead to Bob Motroni, and good wins over Ireland and Wales allowed us the luxury of a last-game, seven-shot defeat at the hands of England, and Scotland were still champions. Later that summer I rounded off the season with a victory in the prestigious Ayr Open Tournament. Traditionally one of the country's top events, the Ayr Tournament regularly attracts entries in the region of five or six hundred and is extremely difficult to win.

Looking back over a list of previous winners is like listing a Who's Who of Scottish Bowls. Past Ayr Open winners include Harry Reston (Deans), John Hershaw (Ardeer), Jim Blake (Babcock & Wilcox), Willie Smith (Galston), Joe Devlin (Auchinleck), Sam Grant (Prestwick), Willie McQueen (Dalserf), Gordon Neil (Ayr Craigie), and in recent years, indoor stars Jim McCubbin (Annbank), and Hugh Duff (Drongan).

*At Ayr Northfield after my win in the Ayr Open Singles in 1973.*

I was happy to add my name to such a distinguished band, but I had to pull out one of my late rallies yet again, before taking victory. My final opponent was a local player — 53-year-old Bobby Getgood. It was a funny sort of game that swung back and forth between both of us. I opened with a single, but three ends later found myself trailing 1-6. A burst of nine shots over the next four ends put me back in front at 10-6.

Bobby then lengthened the jack and it was my turn to struggle as Bobby, urged on by the local support at the North-field Green, edged to within one shot of victory at 20-13.

The next end however completely changed the picture when I picked up a maximum count of four. That seemed to worry Bobby and, sensing I was right back in the fight, I kept the pressure on and was rewarded with four successive singles that took me to a last-gasp 21-20 win. I was reasonably confident that I would find a place in the Commonwealth Games line-up, and with the side being announced in October, I didn't have long to wait.

The side was announced on Sunday October 21st, and you can imagine my elation at not only being named in the seven-strong side but at also being given the coveted singles spot. No less than four of the team were from Edinburgh and the Lothians, with Jackie Christie (Northern) and Alex McIntosh (Newbattle) teaming up in the pairs and Morgan Moffat (Whitehouse and Grange) leading in the fours. There had been a fifth East of Scotland man in the original line-up with Harry Reston (Deans) named as skip in the pairs. Unfortunately, Harry was taken into hospital to have a lung removed just a matter of days after the team was announced and Alex McIntosh, originally listed as third in the fours to Uddingston's John McRae, was drafted to skip in the pairs.

Garry Scott from Errol was moved up from second to third and Mosspark's John Marshall came into the rink at second. The East connection continued in the role of team manager, where S.B.A. President, John Bond, from the Edinburgh West End Club, was named.

While I had been very hopeful of making the side, I felt a great sense of relief when the team was finally announced, and while I knew what to expect on the bowls side, what added to the excitement of it all was being a part of the whole Commonwealth Games squad, and, as a sports buff, I was very much looking forward to meeting and mixing with competitors from the other sports.

A series of practice matches were arranged in various indoor clubs throughout the country, and these served the double advantage of providing much-needed practice in conditions that, while they were faster than we were used to outdoors, were still nowhere near as fast as we could experience in Christchurch, and gave the squad a chance to get to know each other off the green also.

The team gathered in Edinburgh on Wednesday 9th January, and after a champagne reception, we were off to New Zealand the following day. We arrived in Christchurch on the Saturday morning and had twelve days of acclimatisation before the Games got under way. The first thing that we learned was that we would need to change our whole game to suit the lightning-fast conditions. The basics of the game in the Southern Hemisphere are the draw and the drive. The yard-on shot, so popular throughout the United Kingdom, is seldom, if

*With my bronze
medal after the 1974
Commonwealth
Games in
Christchurch*

ever, played in Australia and New Zealand, principally because
conditions make it such a difficult shot to master.

It's not unusual to see players driving with their first or
second bowl if their opponent has a bowl anywhere close to
the jack. We put our practice time to good use, however, and
when the action got under way in earnest we were all reasonably confident of acquitting ourselves well. That proved to be
well founded and we all figured in the medals. The fours and
myself took bronze, while Jackie Christie and Alex McIntosh
struck gold in the pairs.

I started reasonably well, winning three of my first four
matches with the only reversal coming in my third-round clash
with Australia's Clive White who beat me 21-16. However, after
my good start I began to lose games to people whom really, on
paper, I should have beaten. The high point of the event came
when I repeated my 21-11 South African win over David Bryant,

the only match Bryant lost as he powered his way to a third successive Commonwealth Singles Gold. I finished my programme with a 21-8 win over O.K. Dallah of Hong Kong, and was then delighted to hear that Bryant had finished his campaign with a win over New Zealand's Percy Jones, a result that gave me a bronze medal on shots aggregate, ahead of the New Zealander. The silver medal went to Clive White.

Our fours also took a bronze medal when they recovered from a slow start to finish in third spot behind New Zealand and Australia. The best performance, however, from the bowls squad was reserved for Jackie and Alex in the pairs, but they had to survive a last-day scare before clinching the gold. Twelve wins from twelve matches saw them hold a one-point lead over English pair John Evans and Peter Line. The Scots' opponents in their last game were my whitewash friend from South Africa, 'Saco' Delgado, and his partner Eric Liddell.

The Hong Kong pair were well out of the medal race, but as so often happens in these circumstances, it was Hong Kong who made all the running, leading 14-2 after seven ends and going on to an easy victory.

That put the spotlight very firmly on the New Zealand-England game, with Scotland needing a New Zealand victory to take gold. New Zealand held a narrow lead throughout most of the early exchanges but with Peter Line coming on to a fine game, England picked up four shots on the fifteenth end to tie the scores at 16-16. But with New Zealand also looking for a win to give them the bronze medal, they hit back and snatched a dramatic 23-21 win to give Jackie and Alex gold.

It was a great performance for all of the bowls team to figure in the medals, although I did feel that I could have done better than my bronze. However, in the final reckoning I was happy with my bronze and I had taken the first step towards what was in future years to become a complete set of Commonwealth Medals.

I was to take the second step towards completing my medal haul at Edmonton four years later — and this time it was silver in the pairs in partnership with Alex McIntosh. David McGill (Sighthill), who had won both the Scottish and British Singles

Championship in the previous year, was named in the singles spot with the fours line-up of Dick Bernard (Gorebridge), Doug Copland (Perth Caledonian), Jock Fleming (Mauchline) and Willie Adrain (Dreghorn).

But the whole Edmonton trip, in comparison to Christchurch, turned into something of a disappointment.

The first disappointment came when we arrived at the Coronation Greens in Edmonton and discovered that they were heavy — very heavy. The greens were laid on a sand base — the first time I had ever come across such a thing, but help was on hand. Clarie Watkins, skip of the Austrian rink, was involved in green maintenance at home and some hastily arranged phone calls produced a machine that succeeded in speeding up the greens before the event got under way. They really did save the day, and while the greens weren't brilliant, they weren't too bad either.

The main disappointment though was that apart from the Silver that Alex and I won we didn't lift any more medals in the bowls events.

The pairs turned into a real dog-eat-dog affair with everyone beating everyone else. Indeed, the gold medal play off highlighted that, with Hong Kong's 'Saco' Delgado and Eric Liddell, who had proved that their defeat of Alec and Jackie Christie, four years earlier had been no fluke with a great run of results, taking on Canada's Ronnie Jones and Paisley born Graham Jarvis.

The prize for the winner was gold, but the loser would get nothing. We had already assured ourselves of the Silver, and Jim Morgan and Ray Williams of Wales had clinched the Bronze. As it turned out Hong Kong took first place with a 26-12 win, but in the circumstances you had to feel sorry for Ronnie and Graham who had led the table for a long time and finished up empty handed.

Again, a bad start cost Alec and I the gold medal, as we won just two of our first five matches. We went down 27-11 to Western Samoa's Maurice Fenn and Faleve Petana in our opener, but then bounced back to score a satisfying 23-14 win over England's Chris Ward and Jim Ashman. Better was to come in our next outing with a 30-17 win over Bruno Panozzo and Geoff Oakley of Australia but successive defeats from Fiji and Northern Ireland left us in bother.

The Fijian pair, George Thagard and Peter Oates, beat us 18-15 and then John Higgins and Brendan McBrien edged us out 20-19. We got back on the rails though with a 19-16 win over the Canadian pair, and then edged out the eventual winners, Hong Kong 21-15. We added to our tally with a 26-18 win against Papua New Guinea's William Madden and Robert Balenzuela and then crushed Kenya's Harry Smith and Reg Fright 40-10.

The run ended against Welsh pair Ray Williams and Jim Morgan who beat us 20-17, but we finished in style with three straight wins to secure the second of my Commonwealth Games Medal Set.

A runaway 40-8 win over Mike O'Connor and Dave Thompson of Swaziland got us going and we then beat Kiwi pair Robert McDonald and Ivan Kostanich 27-18, finishing off with a 24-17 win against Malawi's Edward Davey and Peter Crossan.

That left us with eighteen points, the same as Wales, Australia and Canada, and two behind gold medallists Hong Kong, but we took the Silver on shots aggregate ahead of our three rivals. Our last game with Malawi saw us surrender an eight-shot lead as Davey and Crossan recovered to go five ahead but we changed to a full-length jack and got back into the driving seat again.

Hong Kong also won gold in the fours, with 'M.B.' Hassan, Robert DaSilva, 'O.K.' Dallah and Philip Chok, finishing with twenty-four points from their fourteen matches, one ahead of New Zealand and four ahead of Wales who took the Bronze. Scotland finished in fifth place, with eighteen points after Jock Fleming, Doug Copland, Dick Bernard and Willie Adrain threw away a bronze medal chance when they went down 19-17 to Guernsey in their last game.

They finished with eight wins, two draws and four defeats from their fourteen match programme. They beat Canada 23-17, Kenya 33-8, Swaziland 22-17, Zambia 17-12, Western Samoa 26-16, Australia 28-13, England 29-17, and Papau New

Guinea 21-17. The draws came with Wales 21-21 and Fiji, with defeats from Hong Kong 28-21, New Zealand 23-22, Northern Ireland 28-6, and their last game reverse from the Channel Islanders.

David McGill also finished in fifth place in the Singles, with David Bryant making it four goals in a row. McGill finished his fifteen match programme with ten wins and five defeats, and just out of the medals, his defeats coming from Bryant 21-7, Silver Medallist John Snell of Australia 21-11, New Zealand's Kerry Clark 21-18, The mercurial Stan Espie 21-15 and Malawi's Cyril Turner, a shock 21-16 win over the Edinburgh man.

It all added up to just our Silver Medal, which, with Scotland so dominant in the home international championships around that time, had to be considered a disappointment, but on a personal note I was two-thirds of the way towards completing my Commonwealth Games Medal Set!

# CHAPTER SIX

## *The Glory Years*

One of the drawbacks of the recent boom in bowls has been the apparent slide in importance of the Home International Series. With big-money events springing up all over the place, the internationals, at least in media terms, no longer holds its place as the highlight of the season.

However, it's still the event the players look forward to most and in that respect I'm no exception. There is something special about joining up with the best from England, Ireland and Wales. The Series brings its own special pressures, its own special rewards.

The pressures inevitably come when you are in a rink that loses, or when you don't perform to the best of your ability. When that happens in normal matches you only have yourself to reproach. In club, county, or even national championships if you lose, then you are the one who suffers, but in the Home International Series there are nineteen other players to consider, and, in a sense, you are playing for every bowler in Scotland.

It is, I would imagine, similar to the pressures felt by sportsmen the world over when chosen to play for their country. That having been said, the rewards are something special, and in that sense I consider myself a very lucky player indeed. I made my debut at Queen's Park in 1966 and the previous year Scotland had won the championship in London.

Prior to that England dominated, with only a Welsh win at Bournemouth in 1957 and a Scottish triumph at Cardiff in 1963, interrupting an English monopoly that began in Glasgow in 1954. Nine Engish wins in eleven years was an incredible achievement but that was about to pale into insignificance in a tartan onslaught that was to string together a world record

40

twelve successive wins and see Scotland take the title fourteen times from the fifteen Championships held between 1965 and 1980.

It was a very special time and one that I thank my lucky stars for being part of. Often, over the years, I've been asked what the secret was of that incredible Scottish run. It is very difficult to pinpoint one particular aspect of it and categorically state that was the catalyst that brought it all together. I tend to take the view it was a combination of many factors.

Firstly, there was unquestionably a lot of ability in the side, allied to the fact that the team had more than its share of characters — Harry Reston, Jock McAtee and Willie Moore readily spring to mind.

Secondly, there was the pride in representing Scotland, a 'playing for the jersey' attitude that made players battle to the very last bowl delivered, and often it was that sort of attitude that grabbed a last-gasp victory when all seemed lost.

Another telling factor was the dominance the Scots established over their opponents from the opening end, shouting bowls into the head, careering down the green to shake a team-mate's hand for a well-played shot and just generally letting your opponents know that you believe you are the best side on the green.

The rink I was chosen with in in 1966 had Jimmy Hamilton (Hamilton) as skip, Bob Motroni (Dumfries) third, Bert Thomson (Deans) as second and yours truly at lead.

Our opening game was against Ireland and our rink won 22-19 against John McCavana's rink, with Scotland winning overall 116-93. We followed up with a 112-73 success over Wales with our rink again winning 20-13 against David Jenkins, and a memorable opening series ended when all five Scottish rinks finished ahead in a 122-66 thrashing of England, with our rink dumping Bobby Stenhouse 25-11.

Not surprisingly the rink I played in was kept intact for the following years' series at Llandarcy in Wales, and although Scotland again won all three matches, we suffered our first defeat as a rink when we lost out to that great Irish skip Billy Tate 19-23 in the opening match of the series. Wins, however, from the other four Scottish rinks saw us safely home 124-72. Our next game was against England and we again drew Bobby Stenhouse, and although things were a lot tighter than twelve months previously, our 16-12 win helped Scotland to an overall 95-85 win.

That set us up nicely for our final match against pointless Wales, but things turned out a lot harder than we had anticipated and our 28-13 win over David Evans helped Scotland scrape home 100-96 winners.

Our rink was again unchanged for the 1968 series at the Belmont club in Belfast and our first game was against England. We were paired with the man himself — David Bryant — and although we were edged out 17-18, Scotland got home 93-90 in a great match. Our next match was against host Ireland and again our rink lost, going down 18-21 to Sid Thompson, but Scotland again won overall 98-88. That really should have tied it all up with only Wales to come in the final match but, as in the previous year, pointless Wales gave us all sorts of bother and they won 98-95, although our rink did manage to break their duck for the week, with a 22-21 win over George Markham. What a body-blow that result was with England due to meet Ireland in the final game of the series. A win of eleven shots or more for England would give them the title and any victory for Ireland would make them champions.

We really thought we had blown it but, even the best sides need a little smile from lady luck from time to time and that was just how it worked out, with England winning by four shots — a result that left us still at the head of the table on shots aggregate, ahead of the Auld Enemy.

The 1969 Series was back at Watney's green in London, where it all began four years earlier, and despite our disappointing results the previous year, our rink was again left unchanged. We opened against England and won 100-85 with our four 22-12 victors over Norman King, and we were again ten shots up when we played Tom Kennedy of Ireland, the exact margin by which Scotland won, 95-85. This time there were no slip-ups against Wales and an 111-88 win saw Scotland champions again, and this time with three wins out of three it was done in style, but we did lose our first match of the week, going down 14-23 to Jimmy John.

So, it was back to Queen's Park the following year, seeking our sixth successive victory, but we got off to an unfortunate start against England in our opening game. A dull, wet, overcast day saw the officials rearrange the starting time with the game brought forward half an hour. Unfortunately someone had forgotten to tell Garry Scott, who was scheduled to play second in John McRae's rink, and at the new starting time Scott was still in his hotel room. It was an unfortunate upsetting start and it saw Scotland lose on four of the five rinks and by 82-93.

Our rink had Doug Adamson (Townhill) in at second in place of Bert Thomson, but Bobby Stenhouse got some revenge for our two victories over him when we lost 18-20.

The second day saw us keep our hopes alive with a 112-80 win over Wales, although again we lost, this time going down 16-20 to Gareth Humphreys, but England also won 111-100 against Ireland and looked sure to take the title. However, Wales did it again with another last-day recovery, and a 105-96 win meant that a win over Ireland would give us the title again. Having slipped up once, the Scots squad were in no mood for a similar setback and all five rinks turned in superb displays as we powered to a 117-66 win, and we beat Sid Thompson 23-14. The celebrations went on for a long time in the Queen's Park clubhouse, and back at the team's hotel, and I was particularly pleased we finished with a win. That was to turn out to be Jimmy Hamilton's last international appearance and it was fitting that such a great career should end on a winning note.

Jimmy's place at skip was taken by Tom Jackson of Lockerbie for the trip to Wales and we kicked off at Aberdare with a 103-80 win over the hosts, with Tom marking his international debut with a 27-12 triumph against Jimmy John. England were next in line and a 110-93 win made us favourites to retain the title and we again finished in front, beating Norman King 22-18. Ireland are always liable to prove difficult opponents. You never quite know what to expect from them and it was no different this time. They pushed us all the way but after a hard-fought battle we scored a 98-89 victory and Tom Jackson completed a memorable debut with a 16-14 win over Jimmy Donnelly, giving him a three out of three record.

It looked certain that Tom would enjoy a long international career, and when we said our farewells after the long journey back to Glasgow, little did we realise that he would be dead before the 1972 season got under way.

That took a lot of shine out of the 1972 Series at Bristol, and Tom was on the minds of many of the team when we took the green at the Imperial Athletic Club for the opening game against England. Bob Motroni had been moved up to skip with Johnny Walker from Tarbolton coming in at third for his first cap, and in a high-scoring game we scraped home 27-26 against Peter Line with Scotland scoring an overall 110-104 win. Ireland were next in line and a 110-81 win set us up for our eighth successive championship with our rink running out, convincing 32-13 winners against Brendan McBrien, and we tied it all up beating Wales 111-82 with our four again in winning form 25-15 against Jimmy John.

Our rink for the 1973 Series at Meyrick Park, Bournemouth had me leading again, Mosspark's John Marshall second, Johnnie Walker third and Bob Motroni again at skip, but an added bonus was me being named as team captain. It was a tremendous honour, one I rate as among my greatest moments in the game, but as I've said earlier, one that did give me a few worrying moments. While defeat was almost unthinkable in the Scottish team at that time, we were all realistic enough to know the run would come to an end some time and I was just hoping the run could continue a bit longer.

Once the action began, though, I had few worrying moments. We opened with a 113-69 win over Ireland with our rink crushing Jimmy Dennison 30-9, and the added bonus was a 96-91 win for Wales over England.

When we dumped Wales 108-62 the following morning the title was virtually ours and we scraped home to our second win, beating Gareth Humphreys 15-14. That meant England had to beat us by at least 36 shots to take the title, and although they did score a 111-104 win, there was never any danger of them

reaching their target and we had notched up our ninth successive title, and as a bonus our last-match 26-26 draw with
Tommy Armstrong allowed me to finish my series as captain
with an unbeaten record. It was a great week, one of the real
highlights of my career. I couldn't have wished for a better
bunch of lads and I was a very proud man stepping up to lift the
magnificent *News of the World* Trophy on behalf of my team.

The bid to take the winning run into double figures was
scheduled to be in Scotland but the Scottish Bowling Association decided to change the venue from the traditional one at
Queen's Park in Glasgow to the Sighthill Club in Edinburgh.
We opened against Ireland and I found myself in a new rink
leading for Dreghorn's Willie Adrain. Another Ayrshire player,
Mauchline's Jock Fleming, was at third, with home club man
David McGill winning his first cap at second. Despite a 23-11
win for our rink over Jimmy Dennison, Scotland lost out 96-
100, but we hit back to beat Wales 104-73 in our second match,
although our rink lost 14-22 against Jim Morgan.

However, by the time we came to play England in the last
game of the Championship, we knew that a win would be good
enough for Championship number ten, and we duly obliged
with a 99-94 triumph, thanks mainly to our 28-9 win over David
Crocker.

Our new-look rink was given a vote of confidence for the
1975 Series at Llanelli and again it was to provide another
Scottish triumph. We won all three games, beating England
91-82, Ireland 94-78 and Wales 99-83, and on a personal note
we scored two wins, beating England's Mal Hughes 25-9 and
Gareth Humphreys of Wales 18-16 with only Scots-born Willie
Murray, now resident in Ireland, snatching a 17-16 win to spoil
our hopes of an unbeaten series.

The following year the Championships were due to be held
in Ireland, but there was a growing feeling among some of the
officials that, with the escalation of the troubles in the Province,
it was unfair to ask players to put themselves at risk and travel
to Ireland.

The Irish Association however were unwilling to give up
their right to host the event, and consequently an impasse
developed and the Series wasn't staged.

We were back in business however at Worthing's Beach House Park the following year, and this time I was moved to the 'back-end' for first time. I was chosen at third in John McRae's rink with a new cap — Hawick's Les Clarkson — at lead and Garry Scott second. We hit form right away and helped Scotland to a 108-77 victory with a 20-14 success over David Jenkins of Wales. We added to that with a 106-79 win against Ireland with our rink beating that great little character Sammy Ashwood 23-12, a 101-86 triumph over England completed a good week's work, we notched our third win, beating Reg Payne 26-17, and Scotland had stretched their winning run in the championship to an incredible twelve out of twelve.

We didn't know then, but that was to be the end of the run, and it all went wrong the following year in front of our own fans at Uddingston. The Series was dogged by heavy rain and it also marked my début as an International Skip. I had Brian Rattray (Alva) at lead, Willie Dyet (Gorgie Mills) recalled to the side at second, and another recall, Willie McQueen (Dalserf), third. Sadly, my first series as a skip turned into a big disappointment. We lost 89-94 to Ireland in our opening game, and although reasonably happy with my own 23-10 win over Tom Sutton, I had a feeling then that things were not going to go well for Scotland that week.

We did get back on the rails with a 112-71 win over Wales, and again my rink played well for a 24-14 win over Jim Morgan, but we couldn't keep it going against England and when they won 113-109, our great run was over and, on a personal basis, I lost my first international match as a skip when Mal Hughes beat me 26-21. However, that win wasn't good enough to give England the title. Ireland made sweeping changes for their final match with Wales; Wales ran riot and a 55-shot win saw them slip in the back door and take the title. That was the final irony as our only win of the week had been a 41-shot victory over the new champions.

Scotland did come back to win the championship again in the next two years, but Uddingston 1978 really was the end of an era. It saw the international career of two great, great players end — Jock McAtee and Harry Reston — and as Scotland were to find to their cost, players of that calibre couldn't be replaced overnight. They did get back on the winning way the following year at Pontypool. I had a new middle to my rink. Brian Rattray retained his lead spot but Alan Green of Castle Douglas came in to win his first cap at second and I had that man Dick Bernard again at third. We knitted immediately and won all three matches, and despite Scotland losing their opening match against Ireland by two shots, a 101-83 win against Wales and a 106-83 victory over England gave us the title again.

My rink beat Ireland's Willie Watson 21-14, Jim Morgan of Wales 23-18, and we finished on a high note with a 31-15 win over England's David Crocker.

Ireland were due to host the 1980 series but again the problems that halted the 1976 Championship threatened the event. However, a compromise was sought and Ireland agreed to travel to Nottingham where the Series went ahead with just a few weeks' notice. My rink was unchanged from Pontypool and we again did reasonably well with two wins. We just got the better of Willie Watson again 18-17, and beat England's Peter Line 19-16 but we never got going at all against Jim Morgan who trounced us 29-14. Scotland retained their title with three narrow wins, an 89-86 win over Ireland, 98-94 against Wales and 96-87 over England.

That, however, was to be Scotland's last win in the Series, with Ireland winning at Worthing in 1981, and Wales at Ayr the following year. England bridged a nineteen-year gap since their last triumph when they took the title in 1983 at Cardiff, and they've successfully defended it at Larne twice, Worthing twice, Paisley and Llanelli. Over these nine years my personal record has seen me win two matches out of three on seven occasions and one out of three in the other two years.

All in, the 1980s have been a disappointing time for Scotland, but in this game you have to take the rough with the smooth, and I do have the consolation of knowing that I played with the best side ever produced in the Home International Championship. I feel proud and privileged to have been a part of it.

# CHAPTER SEVEN

# *World Championships . . . Johannesburg '76 and Melbourne '80*

My third visit to South Africa came in 1976 when I found myself named in my first World Championship squad.

My Christchurch bronze medal had obviously been reasonably well received in Wellington Street as I was again named in the singles spot in a team that included Dreghorn's Willie Adrain, my old mate Dick Bernard and the Christchurch gold medallists Jackie Christie and Alex McIntosh.

As well as the singles, I was leading in the triples with Dick at second and Willie Adrain skip, and, as normal in World Championships, it was the pairs and triples that dominated the opening half of the championships.

Willie Dick, the then S.B.A. President, was named as team manager and the venue for the championships — the best I've ever played in — was the three-greened Zoo Lake Club.

Sixteen countries took part in the seventeen-day event that cost around £300,000 to stage, and from the very outset it became obvious that the South African authorities were sparing nothing in the way of time, effort and finance to make the championship a showpiece.

With more and more of the sporting world beginning to turn their backs on the political regime in South Africa, the government obviously looked on the Third World Championships as a chance to show off to the world. With their isolation from many sporting events, the host country laid great importance on the championships and in many ways it was the beginning of bowls moving upmarket with all the normal souvenirs and T-shirts associated with major events making their début in the South African Championships.

South Africa had at that time around 75,000 regular bowlers spread over seven hundred clubs throughout the country and in a real concerted effort they put on a show to remember.

Without wishing to take anything away from the subsequent championships in Melbourne, Aberdeen and Auckland, the 1976 Championships continue to be the best ever staged.

They were opened by Prime Minister John Vorster who flew from Cape Town to do the honours in a ceremony that contained all the pomp and pageantry that South Africa could muster, with displays of dancing and gymnastics, a parade of the teams taking part, and a fly past by planes of the South African Air Force.

It was all very impressive, and as *The Times* Foreign Service reported: 'It could almost have been Wimbledon except there were no strawberries and cream and no rain. Nor could the J.B. Vorster Prison Service Band be said to play with quite the same panache as the Brigade of Guards. But the three greens at Zoo Lake Bowling Club, where the seventeen-day contest was being held, were manicured with even greater precision than the Centre Court, and the spectators in their white flannels, club blazers and Panama hats could have come straight from a similar English sporting occasion.'

The opening match in the triples was a hard one against Australia, and in a real ding-dong battle we had to settle for a share of the spoils at 15-15, a result that I'm sure pleased the Aussies as much as ourselves. In round-robin competition it's so vital to get a good start, and a draw against a team you rate as a major danger is often a point gained rather than a point dropped.

We certainly thought so anyway, and we improved to win our second match against another of the fancied sides, beating New Zealand 21-14.

Jackie Christie and Alex McIntosh were finding it tough going, though, in the pairs, losing to the Australian's 24-20 and New Zealand 25-21, and we were soon to know that feeling too!

After our solid start, things began to go wrong and over our next twelve matches we managed six wins, one more draw and five defeats. We beat Hong Kong, Jersey, Malawi, Guernsey, Western Samoa and Japan, drew with Israel and lost out to the holders, the United States, Wales, Ireland, England and South Africa. That left us in a rather disappointing eighth place overall, while Jackie and Alex had to settle for tenth place in the pairs.

South Africa took the first two steps towards what was to turn into a clean sweep of all five titles, when they won both the pairs and triples titles.

The South African pair of Doug Watson and Bill Moseley won thirteen of their fifteen matches and finished well clear of the United States duo of Dick Folkins and Neil McInnes, who took silver just ahead of Australia's Don Woolnough and Bob Middleton.

England pair John Evans and Peter Line finished fourth, losing out on shots aggregate for the bronze medal, with Russell and Mal Evans from Wales in fifth place and Ireland's John Henry and Roy Fulton in sixth.

The South African triples side of Kelvin Lightfoot, Nando Gatti and Kevin Campbell notched up fourteen wins, losing only to the England trio of Tommy Armstrong, Bill Irish and David Bryant, who won 25-13 in the penultimate round of matches, but by that time the gold medal was well and truly tucked away in the pockets of the South African side.

England took silver and Ireland, with Ayrshire-born Willie Murray at skip, took the bronze, while Wales (Dia Richards, Ray Williams and Ellis Stanbury) finished sixth.

It was hardly an ideal start for Scotland, finishing well down the medal tables in both events, and while we were far from downhearted, it's got to be said we weren't exactly brimming with confidence for the singles and fours.

As I've already said, a good start in round-robin types of event is essential, and particularly so in circumstances like those in South Africa, and I was well aware of that when I lined up for my opening game in the singles.

Again, the draw could have been kinder, putting me in against New Zealand's Kerry Clark in my opening match, but I did have the cushion of knowing that my next two matches were against the Channel Islands, ones that certainly, on form, I would expect to win.

Clark proved a real tough nut to crack, and the Kiwi went on to move into the administrative side of the game and not only manage the New Zealand teams at the 1984 and 1988 World Championships, but in 1988 take over the mantle of the most powerful man in the game — President of the International Board.

Kerry is a person I respect not only as a player, but very much as a man who thinks about the game, and it will be interesting to see what changes he brings at the top level of the sport, and at a time when bowls needs all the expert guidance it can muster to maintain its recent boom in popularity.

In 1976, though, Kerry's attentions were still very much directed towards the playing side, and rightly so, and a 21-15 win left me with just the kind of start I didn't want. However, I was reasonably happy with my form and I opened my account in round two with a 21-7 win over Guernsey's Roy du Feu and added a 21-6 victory against Jersey's Ben Van Neikerk in my next match.

My fourth-round opponent was the defending champion Mal Evans of Wales who had just pipped Dick Bernard to take the gold medal at the Second World Championships in Worthing four years earlier, and again Evans proved to be the hammer of the Scots, beating me 21-13. That left me with a two-wins-from-four-matches record, and really meant that I couldn't afford many more slip-ups to keep in the medal hunt.

My fifth opponent was the strongly fancied Bob Middleton of Australia and it developed into a real ding-dong battle. I made a good start, though, and seemed to have a cushion of around the three or four-shot mark, then I got a horrible slice of bad luck. Lying three shots, I forced Bob into a drive with his last bowl and despite being off target he careered into the head and when the dust settled he was unbelievably lying four shots. That gave Bob just the boost he needed, just at the right time, and he went on to score a 21-17 win.

It really was a hard one to take. Looking back on it now, I rate it as probably my best performance of the championships and at the end of the day I had nothing to show for it. I suppose, though, it taught me something of a lesson. Defeats are always hard to take, particularly when it's a match you think you should have won, but when the match has ended there's nothing you can do about it — you've got to start preparing for your next match.

It was a much harder, more determined Willie Wood who lined up in his next match against Malawi's Harry Lakin, and a 21-3 win gave me a bit of a boost. My next opponent was a fellow Scot, and, like Willie Murray, he was playing in the Irish side.

The man in question was none other than Roy Fulton who turned into one of the finest players ever to represent the Emerald Isle. Fulton was a top-class player, a hard man to beat on the green and one of the best exponents of the draw shot I've ever seen. He was consistency itself, and after an excellent match I edged home a 21-19 winner.

Roy Fulton moved back to his native Scotland in the early 1980s, but not before he had notched up a record seven wins in the Irish Singles Championship. Even in the twilight of a great career, Roy reached the semi-finals of the Scottish Indoor Singles in 1984.

I was certainly delighted to get over that hurdle, particularly after my earlier defeats, and I kept my winning run with a 21-7 eighth-round win over Rhodesia's John Allman. Next in line was Israel's Matt Gordon whom I beat 21-12 and I then got a surprisingly easy 21-8 result against Dick Folkins of the United States, who had reeled off wins in his opening six matches.

So, after ten rounds I had notched up seven wins, but with five matches still to play it looked as if we were all playing for, at best, the silver medal, with the home country's Doug Watson still boasting an unbeaten record.

Watson was my next opponent and the importance of the match to both of us couldn't be stressed enough — Watson with the gold medal almost within his grasp and me desperately trying to snatch some form of tangible reward for my efforts in my first World Championships.

However, I had to settle for a second best again, despite playing well, and Doug took a step nearer the World title with a 21-17 win. Round twelve saw me back in the winners' enclosure with a 21-9 success over Western Samoa's Tolovaa Siimoa, but it was to prove in vain as I lost two of my final three matches. Round thirteen turned out to be unlucky for me as Hong Kong's Eric Liddell turned in a top-class display to win 21-11, and then David Bryant inflicted a 21-16 defeat. My final opponent was Japan's Shingo Sarumaru, and as everyone else in the championship had done, I managed to finish off with a victory, winning 21-5.

The Japanese provided one of the great memories of the Championships. Making their début in the event, they made it known beforehand that they were participating very much in a learning capacity. They weren't kidding! They lost all fifteen matches in each of the singles, pairs, triples and fours. They found on their arrival that they had to use different bowls as they normally play with non-bias bowls, and they virtually had to start from scratch.

Statistics would suggest they didn't make a very good job of it, finishing with a record of Played 60, won NIL, drawn NIL, lost 60, shots for 421, shots against 2234. They managed to find their way into the Guinness Book of Records after a 69-4 defeat at the hands of Rhodesia in the triples but there is no doubt their presence added a lot to a memorable World Championship.

While I was struggling in the singles, finishing in seventh place, my colleagues in the fours, Jackie Christie, Dick Bernard, Alex McIntosh and Willie Adrain were also finding the going tough and finished with nine wins and in sixth place. All things considered, it was a disappointing performance finishing out of the medals in all four events, and we never looked like holding onto the Leonard Trophy as overall World Team Champions.

South Africa completed their clean sweep with Doug Watson winning the singles, losing only to bronze medallist David Bryant, while Bob Middleton won the silver. But the hosts had to work hard for their triumph in the fours, and despite losing just once they only took the title on shots aggregate ahead of Australia with England taking the bronze medal.

So South Africa completed an incredible clean sweep of

the titles — a truly remarkable achievement from a truly remarkable Championship and, while disappointed that I didn't return with a medal, I felt reasonably happy with my performance.

The selectors too must have been reasonably happy because four years on I found myself in the side again for the Fourth World Championships in Melbourne. Alex McIntosh was the only other member of the 1976 squad to retain his place with the remainder of the side made up of Sighthill's David McGill, John Summers from Balerno and Dalserf's Willie McQueen. This time, though, the singles spot went to David McGill who had won the Scottish and British Singles a couple of years earlier.

I was named in the pairs along with Alex McIntosh and at second in the rink with John Summers lead, Willie McQueen third and Alex again skipping. The venue for the Championships was the Frankston Club and when play began we made a disastrous start, slumping to defeat in all three of our opening matches.

Hong Kong totally dominated our first-round match, winning 29-9, and the United States edged home 20-18 in round two, with Jersey completing our unwelcome hat-trick 21-15 in round three.

We at last broke our duck, but only just, scraping home 20-19 winners over Swaziland and then beat Fiji 25-11. Round six saw a 20-20 draw with New Zealand and then we began to find our touch as we reeled off five successive victories. We began with a 32-10 win over Israel, added a 31-12 success over Malawi, crushed Japan 49-4, beat Wales 20-13 and then just got home 18-15 against Zambia.

The run came to an end when we crashed 14-27 to Western Samoa, but we came back in the thirteenth round to beat Ireland 25-11. We then lined up against the all-conquering Australian pair of Alf Sandercock and Peter Rheuben and after a tremendous struggle we forced an 18-18 draw — the first point the Aussie's had dropped. Further wins over Guernsey (25-14) and Kenya (35-13) pushed us up the table and in with a real chance of the bronze medal, but we slumped to a surprise 9-25 defeat against Papua New Guinea and then lost 16-28 to Canada, and despite a last round 23-21 win over England, we had to settle for fifth spot.

The Aussies duly completed their programme undefeated to win gold, Burnie Gill and Graham Jarvis of Canada took silver and New Zealand's Phil Skoglund and Kevin Darling won the bronze.

Things were going a lot better in the triples, though, and John, David and Willie completed their first eighteen matches with sixteen wins, a draw and just one defeat — a 19-20 reverse against Israel. That put them into a final-game decider against the Auld Enemy, England, who, with seventeen wins and a defeat, were one point ahead.

The English trio made a brilliant start, racing to an 18-2 lead, and they finally went on to win 28-11 to give Jimmy Hobday, Tony Allcock and David Bryant the gold with Scotland taking the silver and New Zealand's John Malcolm, Nick Unkovitch and Morgan Moffat, bronze.

All things considered it was a good start and kept alive our hopes of regaining the Leonard Trophy we had lost in South Africa.

Part two of the championships saw us off to a good start, winning our first six matches in the fours. We began with a 24-12 win over Australia, then beat Zambia 21-19 followed by an ever so sweet 22-14 third-round victory over England. Round four saw us beat Wales 24-18 and further wins over the United States (22-14) and Swaziland (41-9) put us at the top of the table.

Round seven saw the bubble burst when we went down 14-25 to Fiji, but undaunted we stormed back to win our next four matches, beating Israel (26-11), Malawi (24-17), Western Samoa (35-5), and Papua New Guinea (35-6).

It was all beginning to get rather tense as we realised we were on course for a gold medal, and with David McGill finding form in the singles after losing his opening three games, we were bang in the battle for the Leonard Trophy. However, we suffered a double blow in rounds twelve and thirteen, losing first to Canada 20-17 and then to New Zealand 20-18, the latter result allowing the Kiwis to go to the top of the table. It was a testing time for us but we refused to panic and wins over Kenya (32-13), Japan (40-9) and Guernsey (24-17) and a 16-16 draw with Ireland set the scene for a dramatic final game against Hong Kong.

We needed just a draw to take the title and the Leonard Trophy as David McGill had continued his remarkable recovery in the singles and, finishing with eleven straight victories, David had got up to win the bronze medal. Indeed he only lost out on shots aggregate for the silver, which went to John Snell, with David Bryant taking gold.

The match with Hong Kong had everything: top-class bowls, plenty of tension, and the most dramatic of finishes. We led 17-16 going into the last end and the task was simple — second shot or better, and we would pick up not only the World Fours Title but also the overall World Team Championship. It wasn't to be, though, and the Hong Kong rink of Philip Chok, George Souza, Eric Liddell and O.K. Dallah snatched a double for an 18-17 win

So, all the dreams of the previous nine days had come to nothing and we had to settle for silver, and with Scotland, England and Australia all finishing on the same points mark in the overall standings, our disappointment was compounded when England took the title on shots countback ahead of Australia second and ourselves third.

The feeling of disappointment at losing two world titles on the last bowl of the last end of the last match was hard to take, but I didn't know then it was a feeling I would experience on three further occasions.

CHAPTER EIGHT

# Digging for Gold Down Under...
## Brisbane '82

While the disappointments of Frankston took quite some time to get over, 1980 did end on a high note when I gained my first Scottish title — a win in the fours with my Gifford clubmates Peter McGillivray, Alastair Dickson and Ian Twatt. There's always something special about the Scottish Finals at Queen's Park in August, and while on occasions the greens may not be all they might be, it's still the highlight of the outdoor season for most bowls fans.

The Scottish Finals in those days were still confined to the last sixteen in each event and spread over two days, whereas nowadays, the last thirty-two head for Glasgow with the finals increased to three days. My own preference is for the new format and I applaud the Scottish Bowling Association for introducing a system that allows the winners of each district to go through to the finals and dispenses with the old inter-district round. I think it correct that bowlers should be able to head for Queen's Park and the Scottish finals, knowing that they will be able to support players from their own area — it all helps to add to the flavour of the occasion and provides a fitting climax to the outdoor season.

When you reach the last sixteen stage of any championship you begin to fancy your chances and I was more than just hopeful that we could go all the way when we set off for Glasgow in the wee small hours of the Friday morning. I had a good solid rink under my control and I knew that if they played as well as they could, we would have a good chance of taking the title.

Our Friday morning opponents were Dixon, and all the way through from Gifford in the car I kept reminding my players about how important a good start was. In straight head-to-head knock-out situations you have to try and keep your opponent under pressure, and while I knew my lads would be a bit nervous, I emphasised our opponents would be feeling the pressure too!

That was the way it turned out with a lot of good bowls, a few bad ones, and some edgy ones, but it all added up to a 26-21 win in a rather high-scoring match and we were through to the quarter finals where we met the Anchor Club from Paisley and again things went our way with a 24-9 win.

So, it was back to Queen's Park on the Saturday morning for a date with a club I knew well, Tanfield, who were bidding for a double as they were also involved in the pairs semi-final. The opening exchanges were tight with just nine shots scored over the opening seven ends, but we picked up six of them to lead 6-3, and with Peter and Alastair playing well at the front and continually giving Ian and myself good position to play to, we went on to build up a good lead and we finally won 24-12.

It was a disappointing morning for Tanfield as their pairs also lost, going down 11-17 to eventual winners Coldstream, but, with barely an hour's break before the final my thoughts were very much on other matters. Our final opponents were the strong Whitburn rink that had an all-international 'back-end' with Jim Boyle third and John Harper skip.

Conditions at Queen's Park that day were perfect and I ushered my charges down to the relative quiet of the West Green away from the hub of activity around the East Green, the one used for the finals. We discussed the match and felt that if we maintained the form we had been showing, we would win. I was delighted that we were meeting a rink that contained a couple of 'named' players. We had gone into all our previous matches as favourites, something I've learned to live with over the years, but in a rink situation, it's not always easy for your colleagues to accept. My lads had handled it well, very well, but I thought that the majority of the pundits gave Whitburn the vote and that suited us just fine.

When the action began we got the type of start you dream about and after just six ends the master scoreboard at Queen's

Park showed us 12-3 ahead, and really the match was effect-
ively over. While we grew in confidence with every end, Whitburn became more and more desperate, and, as often happens in these situations, we enjoyed our share of the rubs as we
cruised to a 28-12 win.

It was an unforgettable feeling to at last have a Scottish title
to boast about, and when we got back to the Gifford Clubhouse
there were shades of 1967 again, as we celebrated into the night.

Among those celebrating our Scottish win was my father,
and I know there was no one prouder than 'Camshaft' that I
had at last got my title. Little did we know then that a matter of
fifteen months later he would be dead. The end came suddenly, the victim of a heart attack in the Gifford Clubhouse
where he had enjoyed so many happy days. The sudden death
of a loved one is always a shattering blow, but I will always be
grateful that he wasn't subjected to a long, lingering illness — I
really don't think he could have handled that.

The next couple of seasons were relatively quiet although
there was something to celebrate in the summer of 1982 when
I picked up my first Hamilton Trophy winner's badge. East
Lothian qualified for the semi-final stage when we won four of
our five East Section matches to finish two points ahead of second-placed Linlithgowshire.

Our semi-final opponents were the strong Ayrshire side
whom we met at the Pollokshaws club in Glasgow, and we
scraped through to the final with a 92-90 win.

The match finished on a real controversial note with both
sides locked together at 90-90 and only my match with Willie
McBride to finish. I was 20-17 ahead and lying the two shots we
needed for a place in the final. Willie McBride had only his last
bowl to play, and just as he was about to deliver it an over-
enthusiastic spectator decided to give his favourites an extra
roar of encouragement and McBride, obviously upset, saw his
bowl sail past the head.

But there was more drama to follow. Onto the green came
the umpire who ordered the head to be left as it was and pro-
ceeded to return the bowl to Willie McBride and tell him to have
another try! Just where he found justification for that in the

laws of the game I don't know, but justice was done when Willie McBride failed again, although he was a bit closer this time.

Our final opponents the following week were Stirlingshire who had really gone to town in their semi-final with City of Dundee, scoring a 135-87 win at the Townhill green in Dunfermline. Venue for the final was David McGill's club at Sighthill in Edinburgh, and after a twenty-five year gap, we took the Hamilton Trophy back to the Garden County with a 94-85 win.

The game was played in torrential rain and we made a good start to lead 24-14 at five ends. By the halfway point our lead had been reduced to two shots at 42-40 but by the finish of the fifteenth end it had grown again to 68-60. Stirlingshire, though, again hit back and when the eighteenth end finished they had edged ahead for the first time at 76-78. However, we managed to steady and a strong finish saw us through to a nine-shot win.

We finished ahead on three rinks with my rink scoring a 22-14 win over Tom Hamill, and Frankie Gray scoring six shots over the last three ends to beat Willie Nimmo 20-12; Herb Milligan repeated that scoreline against Willie Alexander. Stirlingshire's consolation wins came from John Pryde who beat Dougie Kennedy 27-15 and Peter Lyons who edged out Jackie Greenwood 20-17.

Just four months after that Hamilton Trophy triumph I was off globetrotting again as I jetted off to Brisbane to compete in my third successive Commonwealth Games.

Joining me were John Watson from the Foxley Club in Glasgow, Ayrshire's David Gourlay, Brian Rattray from Alva, my 1980 Scottish Fours final victim John Harper, Sandy MacKintosh from Inverness, and Mauchline's Jock Fleming. I found myself in the singles again, with Watson and Gourlay in the pairs, and Jock Fleming skipping the fours with Sandy MacKintosh at lead, Brian Rattray second and John Harper third.

I was the only member from the Melbourne World Championships to retain my place in the side, a decision I felt quite harsh on a team that had come within one shot of winning the World Team Championships, but I've tried over the years not to get too involved in the politics of the game and leave team picking to those on the selection committee.

However, I was looking forward to being back in the singles, and with two previous Commonwealth Games under my belt I felt I had a good chance. That thought was given a boost as David Bryant, who had committed himself to the professional cause a few years earlier, was banned from competing. It was a problem that was to raise its head again four years later when John Watson, David Gourlay, myself, and many other top players were ruled out of playing in Edinburgh.

It was difficult to accept that decision when people like Steve Ovett and Seb Coe were competing down the road at the Commonwealth Stadium at Meadowbank, and anyone who thinks they're amateurs, to say the least, are out of touch with what's going on in sport. Let's just say that the bank books of David Bryant and Willie Wood fall far short of Steve and Seb!

The venue for the bowls events at Brisbane was the Moorooka club and their four greens were in superb condition. They were under the supervision of head greenkeeper Alex Matthews and his team of twelve assistants who worked round the clock to keep them in top condition. Testimony that their efforts were successful came late in the competition when the Queen paid a visit to Moorooka and asked an official, 'Is that a synthetic surface they're playing on?'

The greens varied in speed from around fourteen seconds up to eighteen and a half, depending on what green and what time of day you played.

I discovered one problem when I arrived and wasn't happy with my bowls. I spoke to ex-RAF Squadron Leader Noel Chester-Master, president of the Moorooka Club, who asked me if I would like to try his father-in-law's set. The bowls belonged to 79-year-old Fred Skennerton, who hadn't played for twenty years through ill health. I took an immediate liking to them and the rest is now history. I went on to win the gold medal and John Watson and David Gourlay made it a real tartan triumph with gold in the pairs.

Thirteen countries lined up in the singles and when the draw was published I was the odd one out in the opening round. I wasn't too unhappy at the prospect, as very often your rest period can upset your rhythm, particularly if you've notched up a couple of good results beforehand.

My opening opponent was the up-and-coming Irish player, David Corkill. In recent years the Belfast man has turned into one of the top indoor performers, winning the Superbowl twice and being runner-up to Tony Allcock in the 1987 UK Singles, but back in 1982 David was just beginning to make a name for himself in the bowls world and after a good match I got home a 21-16 winner.

I then met David Tso from Hong Kong and ran out a more comfortable winner than I expected with a 21-7 victory. Hong Kong have a good record in Commonwealth Games and World Championships but they never got to grips at all with the conditions in Brisbane and finished well out of the medals in all events.

My fourth-round opponent was a newcomer to international bowls, Fiji's Krishna Gauder, and I made a good start to open up a 7-0 lead after the opening exchanges. Then the roof fell in, or rather it would have, had there been one over the Moorooka Green. Suddenly it was Krishna who was in full flow and I couldn't find an answer to his succession of winning bowls, and he went on to score a 21-11 win. It was a big blow, but it's in situations like this that your previous experience at the top level of the game comes in. It's highly unlikely that anyone will go through round-robin situations without slipping up at some point, and you've just got to remind yourself that your last game is history.

My next encounter was against Graham Croft from Papua New Guinea, and a 21-6 win got me back on the winning way; and when I added a 21-10 success against Botswana's John Thackray my confidence was beginning to grow.

Next in line was Garin Beare of Zimbabwe and I safely survived that one with a 21-11 win to take my record to five wins from six matches, halfway through my twelve-match programme. I was aware, though, that the second half of my programme was, on paper anyway, much harder, and I still had to meet Australia's Rob Parrella, Alan Windsor of England and New Zealand's Peter Belliss.

*My moment of glory . . . the Gold Medal is mine (Brisbane Common-wealth Games — 1982)*

Home man Parrella was next in line, but I had studied the 38-year-old Brisbane taxi driver's game closely and I was reasonably confident I could come out on top. Parrella is one of the few characters left in the game — a great competitor, but one who can be ruffled and resorts to heavy tactics if things aren't going well. I decided that my plan would be to draw, draw and draw again and only attack as a last resort, and on the day it worked to perfection as I ran out a 21-12 winner.

I then had to survive two really hard battles. My next opponent was Zambia's Russell Hankey, and I managed a 21-16 win before scraping home 21-18 in my next match with Canada's Burnie Gill, who was to come to Scotland three months later and go all the way to the final of the Embassy World Indoor Singles Championship at Coatbridge before going down to Bob Sutherland.

Swaziland's Tom Green followed and a 21-10 victory set me up nicely for the 'big two' — Alan Windsor and Peter Belliss — in my last two matches.

Scotland-England matches are always a bit special and this one was no exception. Windsor is capable of turning it on against anyone but he had been having a bit of an up and down tournament and he desperately needed a win to get back among the medals although the gold was out of his reach. I expected a hard match and I wasn't disappointed.

Alan went into an early 13-8 lead and was still in front 15-11 as we reached the nitty-gritty stage, but slowly I began to get back at him, finishing with a double and single to turn an 18-19 scoreline into a 21-19 win. It was definitely my hardest match of the tournament, although I rate my win over Rob Parrella as a better performance as I was in full flow that day. That Windsor win assured me of a medal but the scene could hardly have been set for a more dramatic finish.

Peter Belliss, like me, had lost just one match, and we were scheduled to meet in the final round of matches — a shoot-out under the blazing Australian sun for the gold medal. Again I had studied Peter's style and had agreed similar tactics to those I had employed against Rob Parrella. It was draw, draw and draw again and this time the prize would be Commonwealth Gold!

*Back to Gifford with that Gold Medal . . . and a well merited pint.*

When the battle started I never in my wildest dreams thought it would turn out as easy as it did. Peter appeared strangely nervous, and to all intents and purposes the match was all but over after just eleven ends with the scoreboard at the end of the rink showing me 17-2 ahead. Peter did pick up a count of three on the next end, but four ends later it was all over with a 21-7 win giving me my gold medal to complete a set after my silver in '78 and bronze four years earlier.

It was unquestionably my finest moment in the game. The feeling is so difficult to describe as you stand on the presentation dais and watch the Scottish Saltire raised to the strains of 'Scotland the Brave'. It's a mixture of emotion, relief and excitement, but a memory that will certainly stay with me for ever.

What added to it was John Watson and David Gourlay's win in the Pairs. Watson, who had refused to accept the £4,000 first prize earlier in the year for winning the Embassy World Indoor Singles in order to compete in the Games, justified that decision when he and Gourlay won gold, but what a fright they gave us on the penultimate day. Seemingly cruising to gold after ten wins and a draw, they suddenly lost twice, and both times by the minimum of margins. They surrendered their unbeaten record to Welsh pair Lyn Perkins and Spencer Wilshire 19-20 and then lost 24-25 to Northern Ireland's Billy McKelvey and Brendan McBrien.

But it was McKelvey and McBrien who turned into the toast of the Scots camp the next day when they beat the Welsh pair 19-16, and when Watson and Gourlay beat Botswana 36-11 it was a double gold celebration. Scotland's fours side, though, never managed to click and a poor start saw them having to settle for fifth place behind gold medallists Australia, with seven wins and a draw from their thirteen matches.

Women also competed in Brisbane for the first time at Commonwealth Games level in the triples, but the Scottish side of Jessie Adamson, Jessie Lawson and Jan Menzies managed just five wins from fifteen matches and finished in eleventh place.

Brisbane proved to be Scotland's most successful ever Commonwealth Games with a total of eight gold medals won and it was a delighted team that set off for home with lasting memories of a great event.

There was more to come, though . . .

We arrived back at Prestwick in the early hours of a typical Scottish winter morning and a large crowd had gathered to welcome us home; then, under instructions from the Team Manager, the Gold Medals were proudly worn as we disembarked from our jumbo jet. There were loud cheers for each winner as we appeared in the arrivals hall at Prestwick.

And still more . . .

As I made my way back to Gifford I was stopped just outside the village where a gleaming white Rolls-Royce was waiting to transport me the last few miles home, and a bunting-clad village went wild. Scots people have a unique way of welcoming their own, and my friends from Gifford certainly did me proud and it was an emotional moment as I met up with Morag and the kids, Colin and Sylvia, and we joined the celebrations in the Gifford clubhouse.

My only regret was that my father hadn't lived long enough to see it.

## CHAPTER NINE

# *Back Down Under... Mazda 1983*

My Commonwealth Games win came at just the right time according to the pundits. Bowls, as a spectator and television sport, was being widely predicted as the next boom sport and the top players — or so we were being told — would be all set to cash in on their playing skills.

A taste of the big time had come a few months before Brisbane, with prize money being offered in the World Indoor Championships for the first time. As I have already mentioned, John Watson refused the £4,000 first prize to compete in the Games and few would grudge him his pairs Gold Medal. However, during the Brisbane event, much of the off-green talk had, not surprisingly, been centred around the question of professionalism and I for one had decided to see what I could make out of the game after Brisbane.

As it turned out, my Gold Medal made the decision to turn professional easy, and John Watson and David Gourlay followed suit. Watson in particular looked poised for a rosy future as World Indoor Champion and Commonwealth Pairs Gold Medallist but, to the best of my knowledge, he never made much from the game in terms of endorsements or promotions.

John was overlooked for a place in Scotland's five-strong squad for the World Championships in Aberdeen in 1984 and since then he hasn't figured in any major wins although he did go down in the Scottish Indoor Singles final in 1986.

My own future, however, was picking up, and soon after my return I signed a deal with E.A. Clare, the Liverpool-based bowls manufacturer who marketed a bowl endorsed by me. It has always been one of my ambitions to have a manufacturer produce a bowl named after me; I suppose in some ways I saw

*In practice for the Mazda Jack High at Beaumaris in 1983.*

it as a seal of approval on my career, rather like some of the world's top golfers who have clubs bearing their names.

It was still an unusual aspect of bowls, though. David Bryant had a bowl bearing his name manufactured by the Glasgow company Thomas Taylor, but that was the only other occasion I know of where a top bowler had his name used to endorse bowls.

Other endorsements were to follow. Mitre Shoes and Bags hitched onto the Willie Wood bandwagon, as did Walrus Waterproofs, and in more recent years Sports Turf Services, Toro Irrigation and Gaskells Textiles have added a few quid to the Wood bank balance but, while it would be possble — just — to live off the income from these products there certainly hasn't been the commercial fortune available that many people predicted.

On the commercial side, I've been lucky in having the same management group as David Bryant looking after my affairs — Drakelite Limited — and, so far, it's a liaison that has worked well, and I do believe in this day and age it's a necessary part of the make-up of any international sportsman. I know from my point of view that I am not commercially enough aware to handle the contracts and negotiations side of the game and Drakelite have done a good job for me on that score.

On the playing side, I hardly had time to settle back in Gifford after the Commonwealth Games than I was heading back down under again — this time to the Mazda International — a select eight-player event that had begun in 1980 and turned into an annual event.

Under the excellent sponsorship of Mazda, it had always succeeded in attracting the top players and the field for 1983 was no different. England's hopes were carried by Durham's Mal Hughes, one of the best players ever to represent them in the international arena, and a great character to boot.

Mal is a typical North of England man with a real warmth about him and in recent years he has turned his hand to television commentating, bringing his personality and knowledge of the game to the armchair fan. In 1983, however, he was coming to the end of his international career, albeit that in many people's opinion it was a premature end, a view I certainly subscribed to. There is absolutely no doubt that Mal Hughes could have gone on a lot longer than he was allowed to, but he suffered a disastrous series in the Home International Championship in Worthing in 1981 and never appeared in another series.

But England did recognise Mal's talents and made him team manager, a job he has undertaken with the same enthusiasm and success that punctuated his playing career.

Young David Corkill from the Emerald Isle carried Irish hopes with Peter Belliss from New Zealand completing the overseas challenge.

No United Kingdom player had been successful in any of the previous Mazda events, which wasn't surprising with a strong home line-up always evident, and the 1983 field was no different. My old sparring partner from the Commonwealth Games — Rob Parrella — was there along with Bob King from New South Wales, Victoria's Denis Dalton and Geoff Oakley from Western Australia.

*At the Gateway Masters in Worthing in 1983*

I was drawn in the same group as Corkill, Dalton and Parrella, and the venue for the event was the Beaumaris Club in Melbourne, which was in superb condition for what, by that time, had become one of the major events in the Australian bowls calendar. Every match was recorded by ATV for later transmission in sixteen separate programmes, turning the participants into household names throughout the country.

They really are bowls mad in Australia with over half a million registered players — something approaching one in every twenty-eight of the population is a member of a registered bowls club.

The format of two sections of four with the top two going forward to a knockout semi-final is a good one as it allows one and possibly even two defeats and you're still in contention. However, the same principle of getting off to a good start, which I mentioned already in this book, still holds good and my opening opponent was Rob Parrella whom I had already earmarked as one of my main dangers.

It could hardly have been a tougher start with the Commonwealth Games Gold and Silver medallists clashing in the opener. I decided to stick by the tactics that had served me well in Brisbane and try to outdraw him, and it worked a treat. Settling better than Rob, I quickly had him under pressure and of course the Queenslander wasn't slow to bring out the heavy artillery.

He wasn't enjoying much success with his drives, though, and I quickly took an 18-8 lead. Rob then began to get back into the match and he closed the gap to just three shots at 19-16, but a double saw me safely into the winners' enclosure at 21-16.

The other section provided an upset in the opening match when Peter Belliss lined up against Bobby King in a repeat of the previous year's final, but while Belliss had taken the honours twelve months previously with a 21-15 win, it was King who came out on top this time with the narrowest of 21-20 verdicts. It was a real tense affair, so much so that Belliss actually delivered a wrong bias during the trial ends.

Belliss opened with a count of three on the first end but King recovered to lead 17-12 after sixteen ends. Belliss, though, then hit a purple patch and picked up eight shots over the next six ends to stand within sight of victory at 20-17. But King drew deeply on his reserves, picked up two shots on the twenty-third end and then drew three shots on the next end, and when Belliss's third and fourth bowl strikes found narrow gaps, King had avenged his final defeat with a 21-20 win.

In the other opening clashes, David Corkill scored an excellent 21-19 win over Denis Dalton and Geoff Oakley beat Mal Hughes 21-16. Corkill was my next opponent, and with the Belfast man having won his opener I knew that a win would almost certainly guarantee me a place in the last four. However, my win over Parrella obviously hadn't impressed too may people in Melbourne . . . they're great ones for coaching in Aus-

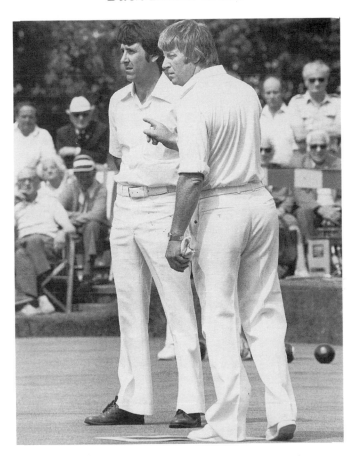

*In action against Canada's Burnie Gill at the Gateway*
*Masters in Worthing.*

tralia, and while I agree that a lot can be learned from adhering to the basic points on delivery and grip, my particular delivery, perfected on the heavier Scottish greens, obviously didn't cut much ice with the purists.

Graham Kinney, writing in the *Melbourne Herald,* described it thus:

> Scotsman Willie Wood is closing in on David Bryant for the unofficial title of the world's best bowler, although many of the purists tend to splutter at the concept. The rotund Willie has a haphazard, ungainly approach to the mat as though he had trouble keeping his balance, but the bowl as it comes to rest has a disconcerting habit of getting close to the jack or other specific target.

Now I suppose that by Australian standards that was a compliment, but my style is little or no different to the thousands of other United Kingdom bowlers. My 'running' style, with my full body weight behind the bowl at the moment of delivery is, I appreciate, completely foreign to the orthodox delivery style taught in Australia and New Zealand, but their conditions are suited to their technique, which generally employs a lot of arm movement with a slow deliberate step forward. That style just wouldn't work on the heavy British greens.

Anyway, the name of the game is getting your bowl nearer to the jack than your opponent and my approach, whether 'haphazard or ungainly', works for me.

My match with David Corkill turned into one of the hardest of the event and I finally scraped home 21-18. David was beginning to show the type of form and dedication that has subsequently pushed him into one of the world's top players, particularly indoors, where he has twice won the Superbowl title, and twice lost out in the final of the UK Singles Championship — the hardest of them all to win!

That should have been enough to put me through to the semi-finals, but I had reckoned without David Corkill beating Rob Parrella 21-15 and Denis Dalton edging out Parrella 21-20, results that meant I needed a good show against Dalton to make the last four. The mathematicians calculated that Dalton needed to beat me 21-16, or, to put it another way, I needed seventeen shots to make it to the semi-finals. That sort of situation always worries me. I think it's easy to take to the green with entirely the wrong mental attitude. You can get drawn into a situation of playing defensively, happy to take second or sometimes even third shot, and invariably it can backfire on you.

I really attempted to clear my mind of these thoughts. I figured it was a bigger problem for Denis — it was virtually a case of him giving me four of a start. My target was simple, a victory, and that would save all the calculations.

Conditions were far from easy as a stiff south-westerly wind made things very difficult, and for that reason I switched to the narrower side of the green and played the backhand when going towards the clubhouse, leaving Denis fighting the breeze, and it was that tactic more than any that allowed me to build up a 16-12 lead after sixteen ends. The next end turned into a real cracker. Dalton lay three when I drove and killed the end, but on the replay there was even worse to come, with Denis piling four shots round the jack.

I had little or no choice, I had to drive again and another on-target delivery succeeded in killing the end again. Dalton again produced a favourable position as we attempted to play the end for the third time and this time my strike ditched the jack to count a single with Denis lying three, but that shot was good enough to assure me of my semi-final place and I went on to win 21-14.

The other section went to shots aggregate before Peter Belliss and Bobby King won through ahead of Geoff Oakley, with all three finishing with two wins from their three matches, with Mal Hughes pointless.

After the opening exchanges, Belliss beat Oakley 21-11 and Hughes 21-9, with King beating Hughes 21-9 and King's 21-9 defeat at the hands of Oakley wasn't enough to keep the previous year's finalists, Bellis and King, from again going through to the last four.

That left us with a semi-final line-up of Belliss against Corkill and Bobby King and myself, but before that it's worth recalling the details of one of the group matches — the match between Denis Dalton and Rob Parrella. I've already mentioned Rob's great fighting qualities, and they were never better exemplified than in this one. With just nine ends played, Denis Dalton was within sight of the winning post at 18-2, but amazingly Parrella began to haul himself back into the battle, and with twenty-three ends played he had unbelievably tied things up at 20-20. Parrella looked set to complete his comeback with a fairytale win when he ditched the jack on the deciding end, but Dalton drew to the edge of the ditch with his last bowl and took shot on an umpire's measure.

In the final reckoning it made no difference to the qualifiers, but it certainly provided plenty of entertainment for the big Beaumaris crowd and for the television viewers.

My semi-final with Bobby King turned into a real classic, and I got a lovely smile from lady luck at just the right time. Bob had the best of the early exchanges and opened up an 8-3 lead after seven ends and, try as I might, I couldn't get back at him and he maintained his lead through to the nineteenth end where Bobby showed 16-12 ahead. It was at that point, though, that I began to see a glimmer of light and, scoring on five of the next six ends, I got back to tie things up at 18-18, and then Lady Luck took a hand. On the next end, the twenty-sixth, I lay two shots. Bob opted for the drive, was on target, but when the dust settled I was lying three with Bob having removed all his bowls from the rink and I was through to the final with a 21-18 win. It was the first time in the match I had been ahead and I felt sorry for Bob, but these things happen in bowls, and I was to find that out to my cost in two World Finals later in my career.

Almost inevitably it was Peter Belliss in the final, after the big Kiwi put his greater experience of the international game to better use in his clash with twenty-three year old David Corkill to win 21-15, in a match that lasted twenty-one ends. The final also gave me the chance to become not only the first British winner of the Mazda, but also the first man to come through the event unbeaten.

The opening exchanges, as in most finals, were tight, with both Peter and myself searching each other for weaknesses, and with twelve ends played it was anyone's final, with the scores tied at 9-9. Then, however, the match swung my way when I picked up a single on the next end, followed by a maximum four on a replayed fourteenth end, and suddenly I was 14-9 ahead. From that point on I felt in command and when a Belliss drive on the eighteenth end missed the head to leave me 17-11 ahead I felt confident that, barring accidents, I would win.

The next three ends were confined to singles, one to Peter and two to me, and at 19-12, I picked up a double on the twenty-second end for a 21-12 win and the title.

The first prize was a gold trophy and clock, worth in total around £1,000, but what really pleased me was that the Mazda title, on top of my Commonwealth Gold, had established me as

*George Adrain and me with the Hong Kong Classic Pairs trophy in 1985.*

the top player in the world at that time, and with the World Championship due in Scotland the following year it was a nice position to be in.

In fairness, David Bryant hadn't competed in either and he would be in the field at Aberdeen, but David's non-participation was outwith my control and you can't do any better than win.

It was pleasing to have won both these events in Australia, as until that time many people had thought that the change in conditions in competing in the Southern Hemisphere was too much of a handicap for British players to overcome, despite David Bryant's World Championship wins in Sydney in 1966 and Frankston in 1980.

And it also proved to me that I was good enough to compete and win at that level. While I always believed that I was good enough, it's nice every now and again to be reminded that you are, and my Commonwealth Gold was my first major international win since South Africa back in 1973, and with Aberdeen looming on the horizon, it was all coming good at the right time.

Aberdeen had been a distant dream since it was announced back in 1978 that the Granite City would host the World event in 1984, and as the championships drew closer the dream became clearer: the World Singles title, won in front of my ain folk — that was the next target in the Wood career.

# CHAPTER TEN

# *Aberdeen 1984 . . . So close to Glory*

If it's possible to encapsulate a career in a period of around three minutes, then I suspect that was the fate that befell me on a warm sunny Saturday afternoon at Westburn Park, Aberdeen in the summer of 1984.

The last bowl of an eighteen-day extravaganza that had added up to the Fifth World Bowls Championships had just come to rest. All that was now required was to decide whether Peter Belliss would be taking the World Singles title back to New Zealand or whether I would be sending a five thousand plus crowd, packed high into the stands round Westburn Park's 'A' Green, wild with delight at a home victory.

It was that most agonising of finishes. An umpire's measure with the scores tied at 20-20 and the prize for the winner, the World Singles Title. It really was the ultimate — a classic case of truth being stranger than fiction. Dougie Donnelly, commentating on the final for BBC Television remarked, 'Had a writer scripted this finish he would have been laughed out of court', and that just about summed up the feelings of everyone in Westburn Park that day.

After I had drawn shot with my last bowl of the twenty-sixth end, Belliss had driven with his last bowl and removed my shot bowl. But Peter had also touched his own nearest bowl and it was now close for the shot — extremely close. I asked marker John Kirkwood to measure the shot, but John decided immediately to call umpire Jim Muir to make the decision. Jim's first attempt to decide the destiny of the world crown for the next four years failed. The new sonic measure, pioneered by the Glasgow bowls manufacturer Thomas Taylor, couldn't provide an answer — it was later discovered that the batteries were flat! Back to the tried and tested tape measure, and Jim Muir first

79

measured the black and white disc'd bowl of Peter Belliss, then carefully took the measure to my bowl, and the big Kiwi immediately leapt high into the air before being engulfed by his delighted New Zealand team mates. I had lost out on the World title by less than half an inch!

It didn't immediately sink in. Peter and I were both whipped off for press interviews and it was only then it slowly began to dawn on me how cruelly my dream had been shattered.

A dream that had started as a distant thought back in 1978 when it had been announced that Aberdeen would host the World Championships. A dream that had grown through Brisbane in 1982 and Melbourne in 1983 and survived the traumas of the ten section matches that left me just one match away from achieving the ultimate accolade.

There is always a great deal of pressure on the host country to do well, something Peter Bellis was to discover to his cost in Auckland in 1988. It's a pressure that, to a certain extent, is self-induced by a belief that you've got to perform well for the home spectators. To make the event successful you need, among other things, a good turnout of spectators and they will only come along in large numbers if the home country are going well and in the medal shake-up.

Scotland's five-strong squad had raised a few eyebrows when announced a few months earlier. I was the only one to survive from Frankston four years previously. David Gourlay, who had also struck Commonwealth Gold two years earlier, was in the side but there was no place for Gourlay's pairs partner, John Watson. Jim Boyle, my victim in the Scottish fours final in 1980, was in the side, as was Alva's Brian Rattray, who had won the Scottish Singles Championship two years earlier with the big surprise, the inclusion of Bridge of Earn's Doug Lambert, who only won his first international honours the previous year. It turned into a brief flirtation with the big time for Lambert, playing in the Home Internationals again in 1984 and then drifting out of the scene the following year.

I had been given the singles spot again, with Rattray leading in the triples and fours, Lambert second in both and Boyle skipping the triples and playing third to Gourlay in the Fours. In addition I was named as lead for Gourlay in the pairs.

*The World Pairs at Aberdeen in 1984, and David Gourlay and myself in the unusual position of playing against Scottish International team-mate George Adrain, who was substituting for the United States*

Again the pairs and triples were the first events to be decided and we got off to the worst possible start in the pairs, losing three of our first four matches. When the pairs line-up had been announced many people thought that Davie and I only needed to turn up to win a medal. Well, it's not just as easy as that, particularly when two recognised skips are drawn together. That's not meant as criticism of David Gourlay, who was one of the best-ever Scottish international skips, but we had never played together at the top level before, and, no matter who it is, they take time to knit together. Our opening match was against one of the rank outsiders in the event, Western Samoa. We were both nervous, despite our greater experience of the international arena, and the Western Samoan pair of Petana and Iosia took full advantage. Repeatedly we looked set to pick up a count that would have given us a little bit of a cushion, but Iosia repeatedly produced a wonder bowl to either take shot or reduce our count.

Even on the last end he produced a last bowl saver that robbed us of victory. Trailing 18-16, we lay the three shots we needed for a win when Iosia played his final bowl. He looked to be missing the lead by a fair margin but then a gust of wind straightened his bowl against the bias and it ran into the head to take second shot and leave Western Samoa 18-17 winners. It really was a shocking result for us and hardly the confidence booster we needed before facing the strong Australian pair of Kenny Williams and Bob Middleton in our second match. Again it turned into a ding-dong battle and again we had to settle for second best with the Aussies squeezing home 19-18. We got off the mark at the third time of asking, beating Kenya 22-13, but we were to taste defeat again in our next outing, and under bizarre circumstances.

The United States pair of Jim Candelet and Skippy Arculli had managed two wins from their opening three matches, beating Papua New Guinea 23-14, and our friends from Western Samoa 28-14, with a 21-11 defeat from Kenya sandwiched between their two successes. But then Jim Candelet aggravated an old back injury and he was ruled out of the rest of the World Championships. The rules of the event meant that the United States could draw a substitute from home country players already named for such an eventuality, and Dreghorn's George Adrain stepped in to partner Arculli for the rest of the championship. The rest, of course, is now history. Arculli and Adrain reeled off eight successive wins, beginning with a 22-15 win over Davie and myself, culminating with a 21-20 win over David Bryant and Tony Allcock to take the gold medal.

Without wishing to detract from the performance of George — a player I was later to team up successfully with to win two Hong Kong Classic Pairs Titles — it was a far from satisfactory situation to have one of your international colleagues playing against you in a World Championship. The substitute rule was changed for subsequent World Championships, where the team manager of each country acts as substitute for his team, an altogether much better arrangement. Having said that, I

*An anxious moment in the World Pairs at Aberdeen in 1984 with both Peter Belliss and myself watching the outcome of David Gourlay's bowl.*

must congratulate George Adrain for the way he handled the position. He really was in a no-win situation, but George, being the competitor he is, played the only way he knows, flat out and to the best of his ability, and his reward was a World Pairs Gold Medal.

Our defeat by George and Skippy turned out to be our last in the event. We turned the tide with a 20-10 win over Swaziland, then beat Zambia 21-15. Our next opponents were the New Zealand pair of Peter Belliss and Phil Skoglund and, while our bad start had all but put us out of the medal hunt, there was still the battle for the Leonard Trophy to think about and a hard-fought 18-15 win was gratefully accepted. We then beat Botswana 18-13, added a 25-18 win over Papua New Guinea and finished our section matches with a 23-16 win over John Anstey and Spencer Wilshire of Wales. That left us in third place in our section behind the USA and Australia, out of the medals but in a play-off with Canada's Ronnie Jones and Bill Boettger for fifth place and we just got up to win 18-17.

While we were having our trials and tribulations in the pairs, Brian Rattray, Doug Lambert and Jim Boyle were carrying all before them in the triples. Their long road to the final began with a runaway 32-4 win over Argentina — the first time Britain had any sporting contact with the South Americans since the Falklands conflict, and they then beat the United States 27-10 and Jersey 32-8, to make it three out of three. Zambia were next in line and Jim's trio scored a 20-13 win and they reached the halfway mark in their ten-game programme undefeated when they beat Botswana 20-14. A 28-10 win over Kenya preceded their clash with main section rivals Hong Kong, and a narrow 19-18 win over the men from the colony put the Scots in a strong position and they coasted through to the final with further wins over Fiji 17-14, Malawi 21-11 and Swaziland 26-10.

Scotland's final opponents also went through undefeated, although Ireland's Stan Espie, Sammy Allen and Jim Baker had come through a much tougher section that included Australia, New Zealand, England, Canada and Wales. That suggested the Scots would find it hard going in the final and I'm afraid that's the way it turned out. Ireland moved into the lead on the second end and from that point on they were always in command, coasting to a runaway 29-11 win that included a count of seven on the fifteenth end.

So ended the first half of the championships, and while we hadn't exactly set the heather on fire, a silver medal for second place in the triples and a fifth place in the pairs left us in second place in the Leonard Trophy behind Ireland, and after an all too short rest day it was straight back into action in the singles and fours.

My opening opponent was Botswana's Johnny Kakakis and I had little difficulty in winning 21-8. That was my only match of the opening day, but on day two I added two 21-15 wins, the first over Kenya's Jim Haggerty and the second over pairs hero, Skippy Arculli. These results set me up for the big one against defending champion David Bryant, and it turned into one of the best matches of the Championship.

As one would expect, David and I have had some great tussles over the years and we know each other's game inside out. I reckon the scores are about even but I don't think we've ever had a better match than that particular Aberdeen clash.

The late Clarence 'Jimmy' Jones, the bowls correspondent for the *Daily Telegraph* certainly thought so anyway. Jimmy, a deep thinker on the tactics of the game, wrote later in *Bowls International* magazine:

> In competitive sport, even at World Championship level, a high percentage of matches are lost by one player rather than won by the other.
>
> Nevertheless, in epics, there are more examples of the victor telling himself, 'I really won that match'.
>
> That relates to the Willie Wood v David Bryant match in the 1984 World Championships, right down to the final delivery of it all; it robbed Bryant, scored a single, and that was it. It was, in my view, the greatest singles match ever played, certainly in the British Isles, and included a feast of superb bowls. Westburn Park Aberdeen was humming with the excitement of it after twenty-seven pulsating ends.
>
> At no stage did either man look in fear of defeat . . . or 'show fear to win', negative signs.

Jones rounds off his article with 'There is so much more one could write, but the match was also a classic of concentration and mental toughness. Remember Bryant did not lose, Wood dared to win — and did so with one of the best shots of his bowls lifetime.'

Praise indeed!

I well remember the match and the winning shot Jimmy waxes lyrical over, but let me take up the story on the penultimate end with me 20-15 ahead and seemingly in command. I played my opening bowls to within two feet of the jack and David drew the shot inside my bowl. My second slipped two feet past and David then drew the first shot just inches past the jack. I elected to drive and removed one of David's shots, which he immediately replaced with his third delivery. Again I went for the drive and was a fraction tight. I got the worst possible result, removing my own two bowls from the rink and leaving David a free draw for three.

Suddenly my advantage was whittled away and with David scoring the easiest of threes my lead narrowed to just two shots at 20-18.

On the next end David showed just what Jimmy Jones had talked about in his article. I had taken advantage of a slack opener from David to trail the jack and lie a side toucher. David then drove with his second bowl and missed, and everyone expected David to stick to the drive, even his good friend and pairs partner David Rhys Jones who said in television commentary, 'David has shown his hand and will almost certainly stick with the drive — he's committed himself.'

Committed or not, Bryant went back to the draw and played the perfect bowl to take the shot before I managed to kill the end with my final bowl. The replayed end produced the winning bowl Jimmy Jones had referred to. David lay shot two inches in front of the jack with my nearest some six inches away, just short on the forehand. David himself had missed a chance with his last bowl when he tried to turn my nearest bowl out of the head for a count of three that would have given him a match-winning lie, but he was well tight of his target. That left me with a forehand draw just to turn my own bowl up onto its running surface for shot, and I played it to perfection — much to the delight of the partisan home support. I briefly thought that it would hold off and not bend enough but just at the last moment my bowl bent and got just enough contact on my bowl to make shot and give me a 21-18 win.

It was a real classic but I had to bring myself back down to earth quickly as I had another match later in the day, and while I suffered a bit of a reaction I still managed to record a 21-15 win over Fiji's Sean Patton, to give me my fifth successive win. The run, however, came to an end in my next match when Canada's Ronnie Jones beat me 21-18.

Ronnie has over the years made a habit of beating some of the top players and this time it was my turn to be the victim of the pint-sized Liverpool-born man from Ontario.

That left Bryant and I locked together at the top of the table with five wins from six matches but I had the better shots aggregate and round seven strengthened my position when I beat Spencer Wilshire of Wales, a late substitute for Ray Hill who suffered a heart attack just before the event, 21-9, while David had to work a lot harder for his 21-17 win against Ireland's David Corkill. The Belfast man was my next opponent and I knew it would be a tough match. I wasn't disappointed and had to go all the way before winning 21-20, but with Bryant just beating Ronnie Jones 21-18 I still held my shots cushion with just two matches to come. No problem in my penultimate match and a 21-7 win over Swaziland's David Thompson saw me line up for my final group match against Israel's Cecil Bransky, needing a win for a place in the final. David Bryant had completed his programme the previous day with big wins over Sean Patton 21-7, and Jim Haggerty 21-8, but I still held a four-shot advantage and consequently a win of any description would be good enough to see me through.

I could have wished for an easier match as Cecil Bransky could always be relied on to provide stern opposition. A past South African Singles, Pairs and Fours Champion, Bransky had emigrated to Israel in 1980 where he continued his bowling career. The problem for Cecil, though, was lack of top-level competition in his new home but his ability was unquestionable. Indeed Cecil proved that just eight months later when he went all the way to the final of the Embassy World Indoor Championship before being edged out 21-18 by Swansea's Terry Sullivan, and Bransky's Coatbridge effort in 1985 is still the closest any overseas player has come to winning the indoor title.

However, while Cecil kept me up to my work, I managed a 21-18 win to put me through to the final. Peter Belliss and Australia's Kenny Williams had dominated the other section, with Belliss beating Williams 21-7 — the Aussies only defeat; while Belliss lost out 17-21 to John Jones of Jersey, but Belliss finished with a shots aggregate of +71, Williams +55, and so it was yet another Wood/Belliss final and I was more than happy with that, having won both our previous encounters.

Before we took the green, though, there was the good news that Scotland were assured of the Leonard Trophy as overall World Team Champions thanks to England's win over New Zealand in the fours final the previous day.

The England rink of George Turley, Julian Haines, John Bell and Tony Allcock had just held on to beat Rowan Brassey, Jim Scott, my old mate Morgan Moffat and Phil Skoglund 18-17, in a match dogged by heavy rain.

When I won through to the singles final and Brian Rattray, Doug Lambert, Jim Boyle and David Gourlay reached the bronze medal play-offs in the fours, we were certain of the Team Title.

Davie Gourlay's boys were unlucky not to be in the final, finishing with sixteen points from their ten matches with just two defeats, losing 16-22 to England and 16-21 to the Australian rink of Bob Middleton, Don Sherman, Peter Rheuben and Keith Poole, but they did finish in a blaze of glory, cruising to the bronze medal with a 30-15 win over Hong Kong's Phil and Edwin Chok, Mohammed 'M.B.' Hassan and Omar 'O.K.' Dallah.

That was some consolation before I lined up against Peter, but really all my concentration at that stage was channelled towards the singles final although when the action did begin it was Belliss who made the best start with doubles on the first two ends to lead 4-0. I opened my account with a single on the third end, Belliss replied with a similar count on the next end, but I picked up a double on the fifth end to be just two down at 3-5. Peter then enjoyed a good run over the next three ends, playing some great saving bowls, and a run of 2, 3 and 1 gave him a commanding 11-3 lead. Even then, though, I wasn't worried as I was happy with the way I was playing and I felt that provided I maintained my form my turn would come. It looked as if that would be borne out when I then counted on each of the next seven ends, three singles and four doubles to put me 14-11 ahead.

Belliss stopped the run with a single on the sixteenth end, but I hit back with four shots over the next three ends to lead 18-12, and suddenly the world title was within touching distance. Peter closed with a single on the twentieth end, and then with the mat up the green and a shorter length of jack he caught me out. All four of my bowls seemed to hang on the next end and failed to bend as much as I expected them to, and Belliss counted three to cut the gap to 16-18.

Again Belliss took the mat up the green and his short-length jack just survived a measure and was only over the minimum seventy-five feet mark by a matter of inches.

However, it was an end I dominated and indeed nearly won the game on. With both of us having just one bowl left I lay two shots and I was pretty confident of adding a third for victory. But Belliss played a great last bowl strike that removed my two counting bowls and I had to draw with my last bowl to take a single and a 19-16 lead.

On the next end, the twenty-third, I felt certain I had won the title. After two bad opening bowls I drew the shot with a trail of the jack with my third bowl and then added a front 'toucher' with my last to lie the two shots I needed for the title. Peter went for the drive with his last bowl and was well tight of the head. But my victory leap came to an abrupt end when he rubbed off two short bowls, careered into the head from an impossible angle, and 'killed' the end. What made it even harder to take was that while Peter was preparing to deliver his last bowl, my shot bowl fell over, changing the angle of contact on the jack

D

*The world singles title on the line … the scoreboard tells the story its 20-20 as Peter Belliss and I start the deciding end.*

*The World Championships at Aberdeen in 1984 and David Gourlay and I discuss the possibilities before deciding what shot to play.*

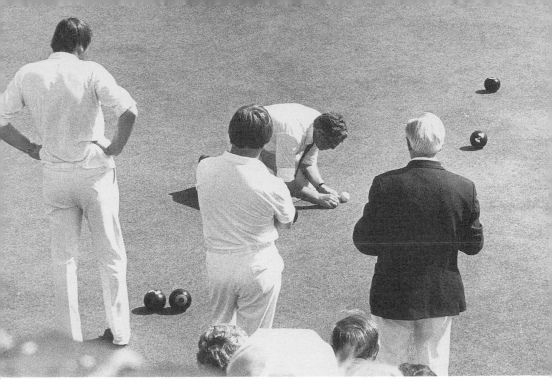

*The measure that decided the world championship.*

*However, there was the consolation of the Leonard Trophy for the five-*
*man Scots side as overall world team champions.*
*Back row (l to r): Jim Boyle, Manager Joe Bogle, David Gourlay, and*
*yours truly.*
*Front row: Brian Rattray and Doug Lambert.*

and allowing the end to be killed, otherwise I'm sure the jack and my touchers would have gone straight into the ditch still leaving me lying two.

Whether I was still thinking about that more than I should have been, I don't know, or whether it was a lapse in concentration, or even tension, I don't know either, but the replayed end certainly wasn't among the best I had played in the match.

After a bad first bowl I did draw shot with my second but missed a good chance of adding to it when I was around two yards short with my third bowl. Peter then picked up the jack with his third delivery to lie two, but they were well apart, and with nothing near the jack I should have drawn shot but again I was badly short and Peter, with no pressure on him at all, drew for three and suddenly it was nineteen all and the game was very much in the melting pot.

As I anticipated, Peter again took the mat well out and opted for a short-length jack which he played better than me. I had to drive with my third bowl and remove two of Peter's bowls to keep me in the game with Belliss counting one. I did have a chance to pick up the jack with my last bowl for a double and game, but with the added weight my bowl didn't bend to the jack as I anticipated and it was Belliss in front again 20-19.

The twenty-sixth end was by anyone's reckoning amazing. Peter drew a side 'toucher' with his second bowl and I was forced to play reaching weight with my third bowl and was lucky enough to turn one of Belliss's bowls into the head and spring the jack.

Peter then played the perfect bowl, a front 'toucher' that looked a certain winner as there were no bowls past the head. The all-out drive just wasn't on and neither was the draw. I really had to play into the head with a few yards of weight and hope I would get a result. It had to be the backhand and I got the sweetest of rubs from a short bowl that gave me the right angle to turn one of my bowls into the head for shot, a real smile from Lady Luck. Twenty all!

The deciding end was a real nervy affair, and I was left with a game against situation with my last bowl to come. After playing my opening three bowls on the backhand I was forced to change to the forehand with my last delivery. I produced a real cracker, drawing to within a few inches of the jack, before Peter produced the match winner.

It was a cruel way to lose any game, never mind a World Championship final, and it's one I've replayed many times in my mind. However, once the last bowl is played it's history and you've got to get on with the next game, the next championship. That was the case in Aberdeen, as I was involved in exhibition matches the following day at Humberside. Spencer Wilshire, who had finished a disappointing fourteenth in the Singles, was also involved at Humberside and we set off early the following morning to head south.

But my mind must still have been on the events of the previous day. Driving through Edinburgh I was oblivious to the world — oblivious until sudddenly I was aware of a car following me. Not just any car — one with a blue flashing light on top. I stopped, and so did the police car.

'Where are you heading for?' enquired the police sergeant. I told him and he obviously recognised me.

'Alright Mr. Wood, but don't travel through the city centre at 60 m.p.h. With driving like that I'm not surprised you lost yesterday!'

You can always rely on your ain folk to bring you back to earth — sometimes with a bang.

# CHAPTER ELEVEN

## *The Indoor Scene*

Undoubtedly the major change in bowls in recent years has been the boom in the indoor game. Prior to the 1970s there were only thirteen indoor clubs in Scotland and most of these had opened in the early 1960s.

Ayr blazed the way, opening in 1935, and they had to wait another nineteen years before Perth opened in 1954. There followed Dundee in 1960, Glasgow the following year and Edinburgh and Aberdeen, before in 1964 five clubs, Bainfield, Blantyre, Lanarkshire, Prestwick and West of Scotland, joined the fray, to be followed in subsequent years by East Fife and Arbroath.

However, it's in the last two decades that the indoor game has really taken off, helped unquestionably by the advent of television that has brought the game into the living rooms of countless people who had never seen the game before.

It was perhaps inevitable that in a country that suffers from the vagaries of the weather as we do in the United Kingdom enthusiasts would turn their attentions indoors, and it was something that they had been experimenting with long before Eddie Ecrepont opened his Ayr club in 1935.

The first attempt to move indoors came in 1888 when William Macrea, the President of the Drumdryan Bowling Club, leased a local drill hall and attempted to demonstrate his theory of moving the game indoors.

Among the experiments he tried was to fit bands of rubber into grooves cut on the running surface of a set of lignum bowls — an attempt to counter the concrete floor — and when that failed Macrea then covered the floor with sawdust and tried again, this time with a measure of success that did convince the doubters that with the correct playing surface indoor bowls did have possibilities.

In 1905, the Edinburgh Winter Bowling Association was formed with players participating on two gaslit twenty-seven yard long rinks situated in the basement of the Synod Hall in the City's Castle Terrace.

It's all a long way from the plush luxurious custom-built clubs that abound throughout the country with no less than forty-four in membership of the Scottish Indoor Bowling Association at the start of the 1989 season and a handful more in the pipeline.

However, there have been some warning signs that while the game is booming, potential new clubs must do their homework first and make sure that they're siting their stadium correctly and in a viable area. Glasgow Northern and Buchan, who both opened in 1987, ran into financial troubles and closed at the start of the 1989 season, and that should serve as a warning to others — do your homework and make sure you have the support of your potential members before trying to open a new club — it's an expensive exercise nowadays with some of the better-appointed stadia costing in excess of a million pounds.

However, I'm glad to say we've had no such problems with my own club at East Lothian which opened two years ago. I was involved from the very early stages, the planning, through the building and onto the opening, and it's given me an incredible amount of personal satisfaction. Before we opened our doors East Lothian bowlers all had to travel to play indoors, with the Edinburgh Club in Milton Street the nearest — not a bad journey in the summer, but not the best on late winter nights.

There had been a lot of talk in the area about having our own indoor club but not a lot had been done about it until we finally got organised in 1986. Being the local bowls personality, I had been the brunt of the local bowlers' complaints about not having indoor facilities in the area. I lost count of the number of times local bowlers had asked me why we didn't have our own indoor in an area where the game was as popular as it was.

On my travels around the country I had seen many different clubs and of course the various ways of funding them. Some are obviously the result of private enterprise, some are funded

by the bowlers themselves, and some, as in the case of the Darlington Indoor Club, are attached to commercial develop-
ments, in their case the Morrison Superstore chain.

Among my customers at the garage was the then Director
of Planning for East Lothian District Council, Graham Duncan,
and I broached the subject with him. Graham explained that, in
an area as small in population as ours, the Supermarket idea
was a non-starter and suggested that any moves would need to
come from the bowlers themselves. At that time he had con-
nections with a company called Walker Homes, who not only
had undertaken work for the District Council, but had also
recently built the Falkirk Indoor Club.

So, with the ball firmly in our court, we set about sounding
out the local interest. A circular letter was sent to all the local
clubs telling them of our intention to build an indoor club and a
steering committee was formed with me as the Chairman. I
was particularly lucky to have a great committee around me,
particularly the man who has gone on to become Club Secretary, one of the local bowlers Colin Brown, and in the summer
of 1986 we got the whole thing off the ground.

The site was chosen at Meadowmill, just off the A1 Motorway between Prestonpans and Tranent, and eighteen months
later we opened our doors to the public. Building started in
July of the following year and we opened in November. It really
was a great feeling of satisfaction when we got going, and
since then it's been a real success story. The members paid me
one of the greatest honours imaginable when they elected me
Honorary Life President and the bar in the club was named the
Willie Wood Bar — I hope for my success on the bowling green
and not, as some of my so-called friends suggested, for my
enjoyment of an after-match tipple. However, I don't suppose
many people have had their local named after them — it's got
to be some sort of achievement!

Our success in playing terms has been nothing short of
meteoric. In our first full competitive season we won promo-
tion to the first division of the CIS Insurance Indoor League,
won the Knock-out Scottish Cup, the Lodge Sports Scottish
Team Championship, and grabbed our first National Title

when Graham Robertson and his father Adam won the Scottish Pairs Championship. In addition Angus Blair won the Scottish Indoor Players Association Championship, and halfway through the 1989-90 indoor season Graham Robertson added the Scottish Indoor Singles Championship and Angus Blair became the first holder of the new Scottish Indoor Masters title, although I wasn't too happy about that particular success as Angus beat yours truly in the quarter finals before going on to crush David Bryant 7-1; 7-0 in the semi-finals and Swansea's John Price in straight sets in the final.

On a more general note, the indoor scene is now very much calling the tune with a fair amount of cash now up for grabs in the major events. These championships are dealt with in more depth elsewhere in this book, but there is no doubt that a lot of the spin-off success comes from the exposure these events give the game.

It's not so long ago — in the early 1980s to be exact — that I opted out of the Home International Indoor Championships. I had only recently opened my garage and with the increasing demands being made on players' time I simply couldn't afford to shut shop in the garage and head off for a week of bowls that offered nothing in recompense. It's a problem that happily, to a certain extent, has solved itself with the garage becoming better established, and I moved back into the indoor international scene in 1986, and I'm thoroughly enjoying it.

My move into my own business came in 1980, but not, I hasten to add, by design. The garage I had been working in fell into bankruptcy, and, with the help of my redundancy money and the promise from many of the customers that they would move with me, I took over premises in Haddington, set up my own business and, I'm happy to say, things have gone well since.

My customers all know me and they're equally aware that I'll shut up shop when one of the major events comes around. However, they're all pretty tolerant — they like to pop in before an event to wish me luck or after one to discuss how it went. A lot of them are bowlers themselves and those that aren't have all become armchair fans, and in that sense my bowling exploits certainly haven't been bad for business.

Many people ask me for my preference between the outdoor and indoor game. I don't really think it's necessary to choose between them: they both have their advantages and disadvantages. What I will say is that with the continuous falling standards of outdoor greens, more and more top-class players are opting for the indoors and it's a reaction I have a lot of sympathy for.

I think we all agree there is nothing better than a glorious summer day with the sun shining and a perfect green. But realistically, how often does that happen? Usually, during an average outdoor season you can count on your fingers how often, and there's a lot to be said for the indoors when you know exactly when you're playing and can plan accordingly.

The falling standards of outdoor greens are a worrying problem and one I don't think is being tackled in the correct way. Little if any advice on green maintenance and care is available from the Scottish Bowling Association and it's something I would like to see the SBA taking more of a hand in.

In fairness to the SBA you can only do what finances allow and for too long bowlers have enjoyed their sport for next to nothing. Sponsorship of events is all very well, but in my opinion sponsorship of events like the National Championships and Country Championships should be cream on top; the event should be self-supporting. Within the last couple of years the SBA have introduced a capitation fee for every bowler, and that's a step that's long overdue. Currently it stands at around forty pence per year, but with around 90,000 bowlers in the country it's still not bringing in a lot of money. If that was increased to say one pound per head the SBA could not only finance their own championships, they could push more money towards coaching schemes and green maintenance.

It's a problem they shouldn't take lightly as there's a growing band of opinion that thinks the indoor could take over for twelve months of the year, and while I for one wouldn't like to see it, I do think it's something the SBA shouldn't lightly dismiss. I know my preferences over the last few years have changed from outdoors to indoors but I would be very sorry to see the outdoor game, as we know it, disappear.

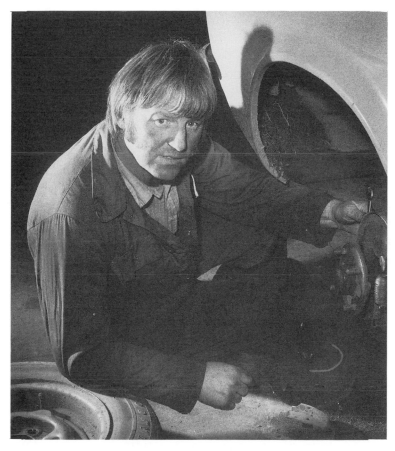

*After Brisbane it was soon back down to earth . . . and the problem of catching up on a backlog of work.*

Throughout my career many people have made the point that they consider me to be a better outdoor player than indoors, a view I don't necessarily subscribe to. My indoor record, both in domestic and international terms, compares favourably with anyone's, although again I was destined to fall at the final hurdle, going down to Richard Corsie in the final of the Embassy World Championship in 1989.

My first National Indoor final came in 1981 when I was in the Edinburgh rink skipped by Jim Paterson with Willie Paul at lead, 'Dusty' Miller second and myself third.

We lined up against the Dundee rink of Jackie Small, Peter Brodie, Lyall Topen and Gary Scott in the semi-finals and looked down and out when they picked up four shots on the thirteenth end followed by a three on the next to turn a 12-11 deficit into an 18-12 lead, but with Dundee 19-14 ahead after sixteen ends we picked up eight shots over the next four ends to lead 22-19 playing the last end where we restricted the Tay-siders to a single to go through to the afternoon final.

Our opponents were George Mann's Aberdeen rink who showed just one change with Bill Morrice replacing Doug Mel-lis at second from the side that won the title the previous year with Bruce Nicol retaining his place at lead and Ian Beattie at third.

We made a great start, scoring on each of the first six ends to lead 11-0, but slowly Aberdeen began to hit back and with fourteen ends completed our advantage had been trimmed to just one at 13-12. A single on the fifteenth end followed by a double pushed us 16-12, ahead but Aberdeen then produced a burst of 3,3,2 and 3, to take a 23-16 lead into the last end where they were happy to lose a single to leave us 17-23 losers.

While on paper it had always looked as if it would be a hard game, and that was the way it turned out, it really was a bad one to lose after our great start, but I was back in the finals three years later, this time in the triples and this time with a happier outcome. Representing Midlothian, I had Willie Paul at lead again and John Slight of Newbattle, who had gone down to Roy White in the 1973 Scottish Outdoor Singles final, at sec-ond. Again, though, we had to battle all the way in our morning semi-final before edging out Auchinleck 19-18 with the Ayr-shire side having a young twenty-one-year-old at lead who was to make a big impact on the game — Hugh Duff, who went on to win the World Indoor title four years later. Duff's clubmates were John Mouzer and Willie Dunlop.

Our final opponents were another Ayrshire side — John McCulloch, Michael Campbell and Alec Connell, from the county town, and Ayr built up a 12-9 lead with twelve ends played. We then put ourselves back in the match with a double on the next end but then panic . . . with my last bowl of the four-teenth end to play, Ayr were lying an amazing eight shots, but I managed to 'kill' the end and on the replay snatched another double to edge ahead 13-12. A count of four on the next end put us in easy street and a further single left us 18-12 ahead after sixteen ends when the match ended on the four-hour time rule and we were the new Scottish Champions.

That win of course qualified us for the British Championships at Folkestone a couple of months later, but as luck would have it, the date clashed with the Mazda Classic in Australia and I had to decide between the two. It wasn't an easy decision to take, but as defending champion in the Mazda I finally opted for the Australian event and my old mate Alex McIntosh took my place at Folkestone. However, there was to be no fairytale ending, with the lads going down 19-18 to the Irish trio of Sammy Allen, Stanley Hegan and Tom Kennedy in the semi-finals.

I fared no better down under, failing to reach the semi-final stages, despite finishing with two wins from my three matches.

I never really recovered from a bad start that saw me lose 21-10 to Queensland's Keith Poole, dropping two fours along the way. I fared better in my second match against Ray Hill of Wales, making a good start to lead 10-6 before Ray snatched seven shots in four ends to edge 13-10 ahead. However, I got back into the swing of things and went on to win 21-16 in twenty-one ends. My next opponent was Geoff Oakley, and to be sure of a semi-final spot I needed to win 21-9, or, provided Ray Hill beat Keith Poole, a win of any description would do.

Things couldn't have gone better at the beginning as I raced to a 9-0 lead after six ends, and after a break for rain I continued to dominate to lead 14-5 after eleven ends. Then rain intervened for a second time and after another delay I went on to win 21-17, not enough to keep me in the event as Keith Poole went on to beat Ray Hill 21-14 the following day, and went on to lift the title with a 21-15 final win over Geoff Oakley.

Going back to my indoor record, I was back in the National finals again in 1987, and this time in the one I really wanted — the singles.

The last four in the singles join up with the semi-finalists in the Junior Singles with television covering the final stages of both events over a two-day period at Coatbridge. Joining me in

*After my win over John Watson in the final of the Samson Classic at Darlington in 1987.*

the semi-finals were two Ayrshire players — young David Gourlay Junior from Prestwick, whose father had been my pairs
partner, in the World Championships at Aberdeen in 1984 and
Auchinleck's Neil McGhee, a newcomer to the scene, as was
Leslie Smith from Newton Stewart.

I played Smith in the semi-finals and after a tight opening I
managed to finish strongly for a 21-12 win while Neil McGhee
was getting things surprisingly easy on his way to a 21-7 win
over young Gourlay.

When the final got under way I made the best start and
opened up a 7-2 lead after six ends. On the next end, I looked
poised to stretch my advantage when I lay three shots but Neil
then played the shot that turned the match, producing a great
last bowl to draw the shot, and what had looked like a 10-2 lead
for me, was suddenly only 7-3.

That seemed to give Neil a lift and he dominated the proceedings from that point on, finally winning 21-17 and leaving
me with the runners-up spot in a major final, yet again.

On the plus side, however, I've picked up my fair share of
titles, including the Cumbria Masters in 1982, when I beat Tony
Allcock in the final, the Tyne Tees Television Top Three, the Ely
Masters, and the Tennents Classic in Darlington where I beat
fellow-Scot John Watson in the final. Of course my biggest disappointment came in the 1989 Embassy World Finals where I
lost out to Richard Corsie — this is highlighted later — but all in
all I'm happy with my indoor record. I strongly refute those
allegations that I'm a better outdoor player than indoors and I
don't really know what people who subscribe to that argument
are trying to prove — I enjoy both games but, as I get older I've
got to say that my slight preference is for the greater comforts
of the indoor version, and as I'm ranked number four in the
Admiral UK Indoor Ranking List, I can't be that bad an indoor
player!

# CHAPTER TWELVE

## *Television*

When historians sit down to catalogue the major discoveries of the twentieth century, unquestionably the development of television will figure highly on most lists: sitting in the comfort of your own home watching major news items within minutes of them happening; enjoying the best actors, musicians and singers without having to leave the comfort of your living rooms, and of course enjoying world-class sport as it happens.

Television, more than any single invention, has revolutionised the world of sport. The major golf championships — Wimbledon and the like — are now beamed live to the world with the ensuing financial benefits to the organisers. Events like the Olympic Games have now been taken over by financial interest with television rights being sold for tens of millions of pounds and of course a queue of ready-made sponsors lining up with seemingly bottomless budgets ready to add their support — and in turn advertise their product worldwide.

Bowls is of course a long, long way from that, but nevertheless television has in recent years made a bigger impact on the sport than any other single item. In less than a decade, television has produced events like the World Indoor Championships with prize money totalling £120,000 — a long way short of the financial benefits enjoyed by top snooker and tennis players, but still a nice tidy sum to be distributed among the thirty-odd players. When Richard Corsie beat me in the 1989 final he pocketed £18,000 for his win while I was left with £10,000 for my efforts, and while I was obviously bitterly disappointed to lose out in another world final, you've got to repair a lot of cars to be left with that kind of profit — and all for ten days' work.

*In action at the Embassy World Indoor Championship in 1987 ... the last time it was held at Coatbridge.*

The development of the television scene, however, hasn't just happened by chance and for that we are indebted to a lot of people. The formation of the World Indoor Council in the early 1980s has had a major impact on the development of the indoor game — not only in the United Kingdom but also in Australia, New Zealand, the Channel Islands, and more recently in Belgium. Europe will, I'm certain, be the next place for bowls to enjoy a major boom. Already they know something about it with countries like Belgium and Holland picking up BBC broadcasts of the major events. Bowls can follow along the same patterns in these countries that snooker has, with the Europeans learning the sport from the box and then wanting to try for themselves. Snooker clubs now abound throughout these countries and there's no reason to think things will be any different for bowls.

Having made that point, I've got to say that I never see bowls getting anywhere near as big in television terms, and also in prize money terms, as snooker. The rise of snooker has been nothing short of meteoric but quite simply it was, in television terms, the right sport at the right time. Colour television suddenly meant that snooker could be followed and enjoyed by those that didn't know a cue from a hockey stick. It was relatively cheap to cover and provided hours of action from one event. But even snooker is feeling the pinch as attitudes to television sport change. The arrival on the scene of Sky and Cable has meant a whole new rethink and in that sense bowls is lucky to have David Harrison as Contracts Negotiator for the World Indoor Bowls Council.

The W.I.B.C., unlike most other bowls bodies who are run by well meaning but out of touch administrators, appointed Harrison in the early days of the television boom. An ex-chief executive of Derbyshire County Cricket Club, Harrison also worked on the promotions side of some of the major snooker events before setting up his own promotions company, particularly to look after the interests of indoor bowls. An affable, pleasant individual, Harrison has brought the lessons learned in other sports to the help of bowls at a time when, in television terms at least, life is extremely difficult.

Jimmy Davidson, winner of the English Singles title back in 1969, is another of these individuals who has helped immeasurably to keep the game on the box. Davidson, a past National Coach, now combines his role as Secretary of the W.I.B.C. with that of television commentator and is another tireless worker for the game. Indeed the formation of the W.I.B.C. is due almost entirely to Davidson's efforts and, with a world governing body for the game indoors, it makes the setting up and organising of events like the Embassy a lot easier with just one governing body to have to deal with.

The Embassy World Championship really was the event that set the whole television scene in motion, and for that a lot of thanks must go to Monklands District Council and the man at that time who was their Director of Leisure and Recreation, Mike Barron. Monklands, attempting to maximise their indoor bowls facilities at Coatbridge, had organised a small four-player invitation event under the name of the Monklands Invitation Tournament, bringing together the champions of each of the four home countries, and BBC Television Scotland agreed to cover the event. Mike Barron, however, wasn't content to rest on his laurels, and having seen the Imperial Tobacco Company add their backing to the Embassy World Snooker and Darts events, Barron then sold the idea to them of adding bowls to their list of World Championships. So the first Embassy World Indoor Bowls Championships took place at Coatbridge in 1979.

But the game at that stage was still amateur and consequently there was no prize money for David Bryant when he emerged victorious from a ten-man field, beating the late Jimmy Donnelly from Ireland in a memorable final. Bryant again took the honours in 1980 but had to wait until the following year before picking up any tangible reward, a £2,500 first prize for beating John Thomas of Wales in the final — small fare compared with Richard Corsie's reward eight years later, but it was nevertheless a start. John Watson ended the Bryant monopoly in 1982, but refused the £4,000 first prize to keep intact his amateur status and compete in the Commonwealth Games in Brisbane.

The following year the title stayed in Scotland when Bob Sutherland beat Canada's Burnie Gill, but much more importantly, other events began to emerge. The first UK Championship, under the sponsorsip of CIS Insurance, took place in Preston, although a strike by BBC technicians kept the championship off the screen. In the event, they missed one of the greatest displays that even David Bryant has ever produced as he avenged a semi-final defeat in the World Championship from Bob Sutherland with a 7-4, 7-3, 7-1 final win. Bryant's share of the £16,800 prize money was £4,000, and television had its second networked bowls event — strikes allowing.

The Preston event, however, was memorable in many ways and really did signal the arrival of the game in television terms. It introduced three major changes to help shape the game as a spectator sport. The first came in the scoring system. The traditional twenty-one shots up game was felt by many in television, and by some of our more enlightened officials, to be too long and drawn out. What was wanted was a lot of pressure shots to keep the viewers entertained and excited. Experiments had been tried in some earlier, smaller events with the sets system — the best of three or best of five each of either seven shots or nine shots up.

The format that found favour was the seven shots up sets, either the best of three or five, depending on what round the event was at. I've often been asked whether I prefer the twenty-one shots up game or sets, and I honestly have no real preference for either. Both have there merits and demerits, although I don't relish the prospect of playing anyone over the best of three sets, seven up. The best of five is a much fairer game and if games have to be decided over the best of three I would like to see them go for the nine shots up sets — as used in the annual Players' Association International between Scotland and England.

The second change at Preston was quite simply the venue. The Preston Guild Hall had been used as the home of the UK Snooker Championship for many years and now bowls was to join it. It was, though, the first time bowls had been taken outside the confines of an indoor club. The Championship was promoted by snooker supremo Mike Watterson who as well as his promotional interests was also a snooker professional. Watterson had spent a lot of time and money over the previous couple of years developing a portable rink that could be lifted and laid in a few hours. A series of wooden pallets each eight feet by four feet provided the base of the rink and each was levelled by use of a laser beam as it was laid. The rink included back drops and built-in floral displays down each side of the rink — all adding to the visual aspect.

The third change saw the introduction of four crown green bowlers into the event — the first time devotees of the crown code had been included. The four were Noel Burrows, Tony Poole, Michael Robinson and Alan Thompson. Only Thompson and Burrows made the second round but again it was the forerunner of greater things to come. The following year saw

*At the Liverpool Victoria Insurance Superbowl in Manchester in 1986.*

another event added to the calendar and this time it was ITV who were turning to television's new boom sport. Granada Television, under the guidance of their live wire Head of Sport Paul Doherty, produced their own made-for-television event — the Granada Television Superbowl. Granada, located in the heart of crown green territory in Manchester, came up with the unique format of pitting sixteen flat green players against sixteen crown greeners, and in addition they introduced women, six of them, to satisfy all tastes. Also, there was the not inconsiderable item of the game's first five-figure cheque, and guess who pocketed the £10,000 winner's cheque? — who else but the man who makes a habit of winning every new event first time round, one David John Bryant, C.B.E.

The following year Noel Burrows became the first, and so far the only, crown green bowler to win a major flat green event when he won the Superbowl title, but one of the great plusses from events like Superbowl is that almost all the top crown green bowlers are now competing regularly on flat greens during the winter and indoor clubs have sprung up in many crown green areas.

Another network event came along in 1986 when the Midland Bank took the portable rink down to the Bournemouth International Centre for the World Pairs where David Bryant continued his habit with a first win along with partner Tony Allcock. Darlington also staged a British Open but it lasted just one year. Television's love affair with bowls was beginning to wane. Sadly the Superbowl disappeared in 1989 although I'm told that Paul Doherty and his Sports department haven't yet thrown in the towel on Superbowl and are desperately trying to resurrect what was unquestionably a superb event.

What must make things all the more aggravating for Doherty is that the last final produced a quite incredible match. Ireland's Margaret Johnston, bidding to be the first woman to win Superbowl, came within one bowl of doing just that before Belfast's David Corkill won his second Superbowl title with a 7-6, 6-7, 6-7, 7-6, 7-6 win in an epic four-hour marathon that had everything — plenty of excellent bowls, plenty of drama, and tension that went right to the last bowl.

The World Pairs also lost its own identity in 1989, being lumped together with the World Singles under the corporate sponsorship of Embassy, and suddenly the networked television bowls calendar was down to two events — the UK Singles and the World Singles and Pairs.

The Embassy finally left its Coatbridge home in 1988 when it had a brief, almost disastrous, flirtation with Alexandra Palace in London before moving to Preston and what now looks to be its permanent home. The Guild Hall really is a smashing venue. The crowds have become very knowledgeable since that first UK Championship back in 1983. Hotel accommodation is within a couple of hundred yards, there are adequate facilities for television, journalists, players, guests and spectators, and the staff who organise the venue are a great bunch — they're very helpful and can't do enough for you.

My record in the major television events is good, although I've never managed to win one. I've lost out four times in the semi-final of Superbowl, once at the same stage of the UK and to Richard Corsie in the 1989 World Singles final. I wasn't involved in the World Pairs that year which in many ways wasn't a bad thing as I had only one event to occupy my thoughts. My title bid, though, almost ended at the first-round stage when I met Jim Yates who had returned with his Australian partner Ian Schuback to defend the World Pairs title they had won at Bournemouth twelve months earlier. Jim, who had competed in one of the earlier Embassy events at Coatbridge, won the first set 7-5, although I recovered to win the second 7-4. However, I was quickly in bother again when I failed to scored in the third set as Yates coasted to a 7-0 win. I survived some real anxious moments in the next before scraping a 7-6 win, but with that scare behind me I was always in command in the decider, winning it 7-1 to move through to the second round.

My opponent was countryman John Watson, the first Scot to win the title back in 1982, and again it went to five sets, and again I had to come from two sets to one down to win. Watson drew first blood with a 7-5 win in the opener, I reversed that scoreline in the second, but Watson dominated the third, winning it 7-2. Surprisingly, though, John provided little resistance in the next two sets, and a 7-1 win in the fourth set, followed by a 7-3 win in the decider, saw me through to the last eight where I faced the previous year's beaten finalist Wynne Richards. This time, though, I won in straight sets, although all three were desperately close and could have gone either way, but a 7-6, 7-6, 7-5 win put me in the semi-final.

There was a decidedly tartan flavour about the last four line-up, with two other Scots, holder Hugh Duff and Richard Corsie, through along with England's Gary Smith. I was first in action in the opening semi-final against Hugh Duff and it turned into a real cracker that again went to five sets. Hugh had produced an incredible performace to win the title at Alexandra Palace twelve months earlier, also ending my interest at the quarter-final stage with a 7-5, 6-7, 7-4, 7-5 win. That incidentally was the only set the twenty-five year old Auchinleck man lost on his way to the final and he completed his incredible championship with a 5-2 final win over Wynne Richards. Not surprisingly Hugh hadn't recaptured his form of twelve months earlier, having had to go to five sets to beat John Rednall in the second round and four sets to beat Stephen Rees in the quarter-finals, but he was the title holder and he was in the semi-final again.

Hugh got the first set under his belt when he won it 7-6, but I won the second 7-5 and the third 7-1 and at that point I felt confident I would make it to the final. But I had reckoned without the fighting qualities of Hugh and he bounced back to win the fourth set 7-4 and set up a decider, but I was always in command in the fifth set and won it 7-1.

So, I was in my first World Indoor Singles final and Hugh Duff's reign as World Champion had come to an end. On reflection that was the one sad part about it, as I thought Hugh was a worthy champion and did a lot for the game. It's so easy nowadays for some of the younger element just to turn up, play their game and disappear. A lot of the younger crowd don't realise there's more to it than that. You must spend time with the sponsors, with the press, with television and with the fans. It's all part of the job, but a lot of the players nowadays don't bother too much with that aspect of things. But not Hugh, he did everything expected of him during his reign as World Champion and I'm sure he learned a lot. Hugh has the ability to win the title again, and if he does he will then reap a lot of the benefits he sowed during 1988.

The second semi-final was a rematch of the UK Championship final four months earlier, but this time Richard Corsie got his revenge for his 5-3 final defeat when he scored a 7-1, 7-5, 7-5 straight sets win over Gary Smith. So, it was an all-Scottish final, or to be more precise, an all east of Scotland final! Indeed, until my East Lothian club opened at Meadowmill we shared the same indoor club at Milton Street in Edinburgh and I had watched the twenty-two-year-old mature over the years.

I knew he had a prodigious talent for the game, having mopped up all the available National and British titles at Junior level, both indoors and outdoors. Richard had also taken over my Commonwealth Games Singles spot at Edinburgh in 1986, winning the bronze medal, and I suppose if I had been given the choice of opponents it wouldn't have been Richard I would have chosen.

The press were building it into a pupil v teacher clash, which wasn't strictly true. Certainly I had seen a lot of Richard but to the best of my knowledge Richard has never had a lesson from anyone in his life — he's just a natural player — but apart from his ability he was hungry to succeed. His UK defeat had rankled with him and he took his revenge on me.

What a performance he produced in his best of nine sets final, winning in straight sets 7-2, 7-5, 7-6, 7-3, 7-0. Things, however, were a bit closer than the scoreline suggests. Richard turned one of my shot bowls through the head to count a four en route to a 7-2 win in the first set.

Undaunted, though, I hit back to lead 5-2 in the second and lay the two shots I needed for the set. Corsie, though, produced an inch-perfect drive, removed my two bowls, spun round, picked up the jack and carried it into the ditch for a double to him and he added a three on the next end to take the set and suddenly I was 2-0 down.

It was a similar story in the third set with me leading 6-4 but Corsie again produced the big guns and two successive strikes saw him take the set 7-6 and that really was that. Corsie was visibly growing in confidence while I was beginning to feel the Guild Hall in Preston a pretty lonely place. I knew I needed to win the last set of the afternoon session to have any chance but Richard again took command and won it 7-3, and when play resumed after the break, Richard wrapped it up in double quick time needing just four ends to take the set 7-0.

I can't really have any complaints. I could and perhaps even should have won the second and third sets. That may have made a difference, who knows, but at the end of the day Richard ran out a very worthy winner. So, my World Championship jinx continued, this time moving indoors, but as I've already said, at least this time I had the sizeable consolation of a £10,000 cheque.

It was a disappointed Morag and Willie Wood who set off for the drive back to Gifford, and halfway up the M6 we pulled into one of the motorway service stations to grab a quick bite and a cup of tea. Inevitably the conversation turned to the final and as we replayed the game we were suddenly aware of the arrival of a group of travellers obviously in high spirits.

A closer look at the group revealed the reason for the hilarity. There in the midst of the celebrating Corsie family was the new World Champion, who had obviously also felt the need for a break on his homeward journey. I suppose it was inevitable that after the way things had gone earlier in the day we would finish up in the same service station. Now while Richard is a lovely lad, the last person I wanted to share the time of day with at that particular point was one Richard Corsie! However, after laughs all round we both set off on our respective journeys home, athough I suspect the Corsie journey would appear a lot shorter to them than Morag's and mine to us.

Opinion has it that the future of bowls on television, at least in terms of network events, is uncertain. But I'm confident we have the right people administering the game indoors to take the right decisions to protect its future. The David Harrisons and Jimmy Davidsons of this world have been ready to take decisions in the past, however unpopular, to safeguard the long-term future of televised bowls.

They had their critics when they introduced sets and now that's become an accepted part of the game, so much so that the Scottish Indoor Championship semi-finals and final in 1989 were changed to sets to fall into line with the wishes of television. Coloured shirts, a move that not so long ago would have seen traditionalists shrieking in horror, are now readily accepted, as are white shoes. All changes that have helped ease the game towards the twenty-first century.

The latest change, in a bid to speed the game up, is to ban players from visiting the head until each player has played three bowls. Again, the knockers will argue that other sports, mainly snooker, didn't change their rules. Cliff Thorburn and Terry Griffiths don't exactly set the heather on fire racing around the snooker table. But bowls isn't snooker and it is fighting to maintain its position as one of the leading television sports, and if that's the price it has to pay, then so be it. Too much hard work, time and effort from too many people have gone into putting bowls where it is today to allow it all just to disappear.

That's why it's important that all the top players do their bit over the next year or so to help the officials keep the game on the box.

Not that all is doom and gloom on the television front. While there are obviously problems as far as network events are concerned, individual television companies are still happy to cover events, and in recent years BBC Northern Ireland have introduced a new Irish Masters event under the sponsorship of Bushmills Whiskey, and in 1989 BBC Scotland increased their coverage of the national indoor singles championship to encompass a new eight-man Masters event, or to be more precise a seven man and one woman Masters!

Joyce Lindores, from Tweedbank, was the lucky lady and proved that she is good enough to take on the best with a first round win over David Corkill. The inclusion of women in events such as this is another change, and again one that has its critics. Women were included in the UK Championships in 1989 and I'm sure the day is not too far away when we'll have them in the World Championships — and why not!

We know that they're good enough. Margaret Johnston proved that in Superbowl, and in other televised events players
like Joyce Lindores, Norma Shaw and Julie Davies have had
their moments. Once players get over the shock of having to
play women in the major events, things will be a lot better. I
know a lot of men don't like it. They feel it puts them under
added pressure, but like the rest of the changes made for television they have to be lived with — it's no disgrace to lose to
players of the calibre of Margaret Johnston, Joyce Lindores,
Norma Shaw or Julie Davies, once players accept them for
their bowling ability and forget they're women.

What a lot of club bowlers don't realise is that they too
benefit from the big television events. The W.I.B.C. run the
events, make a healthy profit from each one, and plough that
money back into the game through their respective national
associations. That is one of the big differences from snooker,
where little or no money is syphoned off to support the grass
roots of the game. I get really annoyed when some club bowlers complain that the game is run for the top players. While I
don't deny there's a nice bit of money about now, all the top
players are helping the game at club level too and the W.I.B.C.
are administering the game with everyone's interests in mind
— not just the lucky few whose faces pop up on the box at regular intervals.

# CHAPTER THIRTEEN

## *New Zealand*

With the World Championships coming round only every four years I had a long time to wait before planning my next outdoor campaign. Aberdeen, and my defeat from Peter Belliss, still rankled. However, when the team was announced for the Sixth World Championships in New Zealand in February 1988, I was given a chance by the Scottish Bowling Association to obliterate that memory. I was again named in the single spot. Joining me on the trip to Auckland were Commonwealth Games Pairs Gold Medallists Grant Knox from Armadale and Dreghorn's George Adrain and two east-coast colleagues, Willie Paul from Tanfield and my old mate Alec McIntosh from Newbattle. As expected, Knox and Adrain were named in the pairs and I was in the middle spot in the triples with Willie Paul at lead and 'Big Ec' skip. The fours line-up had Willie at lead, Grant Knox second, George Adrain third and Alec skip.

The venue chosen by the New Zealand Bowling Association was the Henderson Bowling Club, a new four-green complex that had only been built some seven years earlier, specifically to host the 1988 event. There had been a major move to hold the Championship in Christchurch, but Auckland, with around one-third of New Zealand's three million population, had carried the day.

Playing conditions in New Zealand are totally foreign to anything in the United Kingdom. The playing surface is cotula weed and greens can run at anything up to twenty-odd seconds with the norm around eighteen or nineteen seconds, and that in itself was the first problem we encountered. The greens weren't as fast as we had expected, around fifteen seconds, and the condition of the greens were, frankly, a big disappoint-

*Before the action began in Auckland, and Tony Allcock, David Bryant, Stan Espie and yours truly plan our campaigns with a quick look through the programme.*

ment. They were nowhere near level and weren't as good as our own at Westburn Park four years earlier.

I didn't hide my opinion of the Henderson greens and I don't suppose it went down too well with some of the locals. After I lost out to David Bryant in the singles final I was accused in the local press of 'sour grapes', but now, almost two years later, I still stand by my comments. By any standards, and New Zealand's in particular, the greens were disappointing.

An added problem for British players was the dates for the championships — right in the middle of the indoor season — and with the World Indoor Championship and its £75,000 prize money just a few weeks away, it wasn't the best preparation for either event, having to chop and change between indoor and outdoor conditions.

Defending singles champion Peter Belliss, playing on his home patch, was widely expected to retain his title, but long

*In action at*
*Henderson*

before the end of the singles Belliss was beginning to feel the pressure of playing in front of his home crowd, and New Zealanders are notoriously fickle — they expect winners and don't like to settle for anything less.

As usual the pairs and triples were the first events to be decided and Willie, Alec and I made a good start in the triples. We had just one match on the opening day, following on the opening ceremony where all twenty-three countries paraded onto the green behind their national flags. Botswana's Mel David, John Baylis and John Thackray provided the opposition and we had a comfortable 22-9 win. On the second day we faced Ricardo Cantarini, Julian Daunevig and Enrri Merli of

Argentina and managed a 27-11 win before going on to beat Israel's Joe Goldberg, Cecil Cooper and Sam Skudowitz 25-13. Next in line were Phillip Rei, Derek Penny and Tau Nancie from Papua New Guinea and a 21-13 win gave us a four out of four start. The run came to an end, however, in our next game when Zimbabwe's Richard Hayden, Bill Cumming and Paul Kramer beat us 21-15.

We immediately got back on the winning way on day four, getting the best of a high-scoring encounter with Zambia's Japie Van Deventer, Corrie Krige and Tom Powell to win 28-20, and we kept up the good work with a 24-12 success over Kenya's Richard Dugdale, Oliver Fowler and John Bone. The following day we had just one match and we beat Hong Kong's Noel Kennedy, Danny Ho and David Tso 22-11, and then enjoyed a rest session in the afternoon knowing we were bang on course for a place in the final, needing just one win from either of our last two matches against Swaziland or Jersey.

As it turned out, it was just as well we had a bit of a cushion over our rivals as we struggled in both our last-day encounters. Nothing would go right against Swaziland and Hayley Abrahams, Derek James and Dave Thompson severely dented our title hopes with a 23-14 win. That left us in a straight battle with Jersey's Brian Attwood, Paul James and Tim Mallet with the prize for the winner a place in the final. We went into the game one point ahead of the Channel Islanders and a draw would be good enough for us. Not surprisingly it turned into a low-scoring, tense battle but we always seemed to be just in control and a 17-14 win put us through to the final.

There is no doubt the draw had favoured us with the other section a veritable minefield of potential disasters, with England, New Zealand, Australia, holders Ireland and Wales all grouped together. It was hosts New Zealand who finally won through with their side of Ian Dickison, Morgan Moffat and Phil Skoglund qualifying from their eleven-match section with nine wins and one draw. The draw came in their opening match with Jim Morgan's Welsh triple and their only defeat came when they lost 24-13 to the United States side of Neil McInnes, Skippy Arculli and Frank Souza. They had a couple of close-

*The Triples Final and Willie Paul and myself watch anxiously an effort from Alec McIntosh.*

E

*A near miss in the
Triples final against
New Zealand*

run things, just edging out John Bell's England triple 15-14 and
Darby Ross's Australian team 17-15, but it was New Zealand
who joined us in the final.

The home side lined up very much as favourites but we
were reasonably confident and, scoring on four of the first five
ends, including a four on the fifth end, we opened up an 8-2
lead. The Kiwi's, though, urged on by the home support, hit
back, and a count of three on the ninth end saw them close the
gap to be only one down at 9-8. We picked up a double on the
next end, the tenth, but back came Skoglund with a three and a
single to push New Zealand ahead for the first time at 12-11,

*Silver again . . . with Willie Paul and Alec McIntosh at the Medal
Presentation Ceremony for the Triples in Auckland.*

after twelve ends. But their lead was short-lived as we grabbed
a double to lead 13-12. The next three ends were confined to
singles with us scoring two of them and, with two ends to play,
we were 15-13 ahead. Then it all went wrong. We lost a three on
the seventeenth end to drop behind again, and then lost two
more on the last end to leave New Zealand 18-15 winners.

In retrospect, I reckon we played the wrong shot on the last
end. We tried to play the perfect shot when perhaps the drive to
kill the end would have been easier. When I failed to draw with
my first bowl, we should have gone for the strike with my next
two bowls and Alec's three — giving us five attempts to kill it
and force a replayed end. It is of course a lot easier in hindsight,
and had we got the shot with our draw I would have been sure
that was the right shot to play.

Anyway, the bottom line was that I had lost out on another
sore one! Almost everyone who saw the final reckoned that we
had produced the best team performance but Phil Skoglund
had an incredible game and played three or four conversion
shots that were worthy of winning any game. What added to
the disappointment was that I had promised my mother Jenny,

who was ill in hospital, that I would bring her back a medal. I did, but once again, it was the wrong colour!

New Zealand's win made them favourites to take the Leonard Trophy as Rowan Brassey and Peter Belliss also won the pairs. They had powered their way through to the final with an eleven out of eleven record in their section matches including a 21-15 win over Grant Knox and George Adrain. That was Scotland's first reverse in the event, but defeats in their last two games against Papua New Guinea and Hong Kong pushed them down to third place in their section and a 22-15 win over Israel's Gordon Seef and Cecil Bransky in the cross-ties gave them fifth place.

The pairs final turned into a fascinating clash with the New Zealanders facing David Bryant and Tony Allcock with the English pair desperate to erase the memory of their single-shot defeat from Skippy Arculli and George Adrain four years earlier. The match developed into a tremendous leads battle with Brassey and Bryant producing a succession of perfect draws and precision drives when the head appeared to be going against them.

It was Brassey and Belliss, though, who were producing the fireworks. After dropping a single on the opening end they restricted England to just one more count, a double on the eighth as they raced to a 14-3, twelve end lead. But then England began their fightback with a five on the thirteenth end, and it continued as they hauled themselves back to be only three shots down at 15-12 with sixteen ends played. New Zealand, though, held firm and picked up three successive singles to stretch their advantage to 18-12, and even when Bryant and Allcock scored a single on the penultimate end the Kiwi's were happy to play out the last end with a five-shot cushion, restricting the English pair to a three for an 18-16 victory.

So, the opening part of the Sixth World Championships belonged very firmly to hosts New Zealand and the United Kingdom challenge had, so far anyway, been repelled.

However, there was no chance either to reflect on the opening exchanges or plan for the forthcoming battles as the singles and fours began the following day. That is one of the problems of the outdoor World Championships with a lot of bowls having to be crammed into a short space of time. With around twenty-three teams competing, the cost of an extra day adds up to a lot of money and consequently, while it would be nice to have a day, or even two, between the different events it's not really a realistic proposition. The 1988 Championships were fortunate to secure an excellent sponsor in the Bank of New Zealand who funded them to the extent of three-quarters of a million $NZ — around £300,000 sterling. Another innovation in Auckland was the use of coloured shirt trim to match the players' bowls discs — the first time the World Championships had strayed from the traditional all white, and the singles matches would be played to twenty-five shots up, a sort of halfway house introduced by the International Bowling Board in their bid to standardise the game worldwide with the game in Britain played on twenty-one up and in Australia thirty-one up.

I was reasonably happy with my section which included Australia's Kenny Williams, Cecil Bransky from Israel, young Robert Weale of Wales and Canada's Alf Wallace, who I figured would cause me my biggest problems. Wallace was my first opponent. Born in Bridge of Allan, Wallace had played in a Scottish International trial before emigrating to Canada in 1980, making an immediate impact with a win in the Canadian Singles the following year, and he had finished fourth in the Singles in the Edinburgh Commonwealth Games two years earlier. I knew it would be a hard test and it was, but I got home 25-20 and we were on the road again. But what a shock was in store for me in my next match later in the day.

My opponent was Joe Riveros, a thirty-seven year old financial consultant from Buenos Aires. Argentina, in world bowls terms, are completely unrated, but Joe provided the upset of the championship when he beat me 25-24. The after-match press conference was also rather unusual as I suspect it was the first time ever in the history of bowls that it was conducted in Spanish through an interpreter!

I was bitterly disappointed at losing to Riveros. It offset the benefit of my good result against Wallace, but the advantage was that, with respect, Joe wasn't really a medal prospect. I knew he would lose games and if I kept on winning, I would still be in the shake-up, but, equally, I knew I couldn't afford any more silly slip-ups.

Cecil Bransky was my next opponent and he too had suffered a first-day defeat, losing 25-16 to Kenny Williams, before reversing that scoreline against Robert Weale. That made our match all the more vital, with the loser facing an uphill battle to stay in contention. I played well, though, and was very happy to leave the green with a 25-14 win and I completed a good day's work with a 25-12 win over Fiji's Peter Fong. On day three I had just one scheduled match — against Swaziland's Bob Elliott — and a runaway 25-4 win allowed me to enjoy my afternoon rest session with a four out of five record — the same as Kenny Williams who was beginning to emerge as my main section rival.

On the fourth day both Kenny and I added two wins each. I beat Mike Nicolle of Guernsey 25-11 and Botswana's Mel David 25-16, while Williams also beat Mel David and my first-day conqueror Joe Riveros, and with three matches to play it was looking more and more as if it would be all down to when we met each other the following afternoon. Before then I had to face Kenya's Brian Jennings, while Kenny's opponent was Swaziland's Bob Elliott and we both notched up 25-10 wins to set up the much heralded section decider!

It turned into a nightmare for me, and, no matter what I tried, I couldn't shake off Williams who always seemed to have the edge and a 25-18 win left the Aussie as hot favourite to go through to the final. All he needed was a victory over Mike Nicolle, or even a narrow defeat would be good enough, provided I didn't score a runaway win over Robert Weale. This time, though, it was Williams's turn for the nightmare.

I had sought out Mike Nicolle the previous night and told him he was good enough to beat Kenny. I've known Mike for years and know that on his day he's a match for anyone. His problem is a lack of consistency — he can't produce ten or eleven good performances in a World Championship or Commonwealth Games situation but he is more than capable of a result against the best. My pep talk certainly seemed to do the trick. It was Mike who called the shots from the opening and it was Kenny's turn to run through the little spaces between jack and bowl, and the longer the game went, the more one could sense Kenny's frustration was beginning to get to him, and the Channel Islander threw me the lifeline I wanted with a 25-13 win. While all this drama was unfolding, I was battling away against Robert Weale just a couple of rinks away from the Nicolle-Williams encounter.

It was a difficult position. I knew I must beat Robert to have any chance and it was a real test of character to keep my mind on the immediate problem and try to shut myself off from the Nicolle-Williams clash. You can't afford to take liberties with anyone in World Championships and Robert Weale was a very dangerous opponent. One of the few top-class United Kingdom players who doesn't play indoors — he has no indoor club within easy reach of his Presteigne home — Robert burst on the scene in 1984 when he skipped his father and two brothers to the Welsh fours title, the same year he made his World Championship début in Aberdeen.

Anyway, I always seemed to have the edge but, not long after Mike Nicolle finished his match with Kenny Williams, I was right in the thick of it, tied at 20-20 as Robert mounted a counter-attack. However, having already thrown away one chance of securing a final place, I was in no mood to do it again, and I scored on the next three ends for a 25-20 win and I was in the final again.

The other final spot had been decided the previous day with David Bryant putting himself in an unassailable position with ten straight wins and Bryant finished his programme in style with a 25-22 win over Ireland's Stan Espie to make it an amazing eleven wins from eleven matches.

Defending champion Peter Belliss could manage no better than fifth place after a distastrous start that saw him lose four successive afternoon matches — to Zambia's Andy Taylor, Stan Espie, eventual bronze medallist Garin Beare from Zimbabwe and Bryant, who served notice of his title intentions with a 25-12 win.

So, it was old rival David Bryant and me for the World Title!

While the singles battles were raging, Willie Paul, Grant Knox, George Adrain and Alec McIntosh were enjoying a good fours championship, finishing their programme with nine wins from eleven matches and third place in their section behind Ireland's Rodney McCutcheon, John McCloughlin, Sammy Allen and Jim Baker and Tony Allcock's England side. Only a last-match 22-20 defeat from Ireland kept Scotland out of the final and they had to settle for sixth spot when Australia won the cross-tie 31-14 while Ireland went on to take the title with a 26-15 win over New Zealand.

Undefeated Bryant lined up as very much the favourite and that suited me just fine. I began with a double on the first end but David replied with two singles and a double to lead 4-2. Then, though, I really took a grip on the final, and scoring on nine out of the next ten ends I jumped into a commanding 14-5 lead. Back came David with a burst of 2, 3, and 2 to cut my advantage to 14-12, but a single followed by a double and a full house pushed me clear again at 21-12.

I've been asked since then if the thought went through my mind that had they kept the Championships at twenty-one up I would have been World Champion, but I can honestly say it didn't occur to me — I was just thinking about getting to twenty-five. The pendulum then swung to David and an uninterrupted run of ten shots saw him edge 22-21 ahead. I halted the run, though, with a single on the twenty-seventh end to square at twenty-two all and then the rain clouds that had been gathering over the Henderson green opened up with a vengeance. Within seconds the green was awash and we were all forced into the sanctuary of the clubhouse.

The rain couldn't have come at a worse time. I had been scoring my shots at a long length jack while David had me on the run with the short ones. When I scored on the twenty-seventh end I was desperate for the rain to stay off and let me get back to the longer length. The delay lasted around fifty minutes before we eventually got back onto the green and it was all over in just one more end. Despite playing what I consider a perfect end, I lost three shots and with it another chance at a world title.

*David Bryant delivers during the Singles Final.*

After four deliveries I lay two with David having played his two bowls some four feet past the jack. I elected to cover his two bowls and played it perfectly, splitting them and nestling between them. David drove, and took off both my counting shots. I again drew shot with my last bowl and again David went for a strike. He was bang on target, but even he didn't think possible the result he got, forcing them both off the rink, and when his last bowl stayed in play he counted a three with the only bowls left on the green.

David admitted later he went for the shot hoping to get one — 'It never entered my head that I would end up with three,' he admitted.

To say I was disappointed was an understatement, I was devastated. My immediate reaction in the press room later was to say — 'I'm destined never to win — it's fate — but what can you do?'

Since then, however, I've mellowed a bit. I don't know if I'll be in the team in 1992 for the next championships at Worthing, let alone be in the singles, but if I am I'll be giving it all I've got — just like I did in both Aberdeen and Auckland.

That left me with two silver medals from New Zealand and we also took third place in the Leonard Trophy with England taking first place and New Zealand, despite their great start, having to settle for second place, paying dearly for Peter Belliss's ninth spot in the Singles.

I couldn't help but feel sorry for Peter. As I've said earlier, New Zealanders don't like losers and despite his win in the pairs with Rowan Brassey, a lot of the Kiwis felt Peter had let them down because he didn't retain his singles crown which was, to say the least, unfair.

# CHAPTER FOURTEEN

## *Back to Commonwealth Action*

When the rules on professionalism ruled me out of the 1986 Commonwealth Games and robbed me of the chance to defend my Singles title in front of my ain folk, I have to confess that I thought I had seen the last of the action in the Commonwealth Games.

However, as I'm learning more and more, nothing, particularly in bowls, is forever. David Bryant, Tony Allcock and myself had all been ruled out of the Balgreen action as we had been declared professionals, but since then the International Bowling Board have redefined their definition of the word 'amateur'.

The International Bowling Board have in their wisdom decreed that 'all players are eligible for selection for Commonwealth Games except those whose principal source of income is derived from playing the game of bowls'.

While it's hardly the most definitive of judgements, it did allow me to come back into the reckoning for the team for Auckland in 1990, and as it turned out Bryant and Allcock were also back in action, claiming with some justification that they earn more as directors of their own companies than they do from 'playing bowls'. The relevant point appears to be that endorsing and selling equipment and talking and writing about bowls does not, in the eyes of the International Bowling Board, count.

Anyway, the important point as far as I was concerned was that I was back in the Commonwealth Games reckoning and in with a chance of adding to my set of medals I had completed with Gold in Brisbane.

The Games were scheduled for late January 1990, and when the side was announced I was in action again, but not in the Singles. That berth went to Richard Corsie who had won the Bronze Medal in Edinburgh. I was given the skips spot in the fours, with George Adrain who had won a Pairs Gold at Balgreen with Grant Knox, named as third. Denis Love from Dumfries, who had returned to the Internatinal side at Worthing in the summer, was named at lead, with Aberdeen Northern's Ian Bruce at second.

The pairs spot went to two of my East Lothian Indoor clubmates, Graham Robertson from Tranent and Haddington's Angus Blair. The women's side had Senga McCrone from Hawick Buccleuch in the Singles, Annbank's Sarah Gourlay and Frances Whyte from Priorscroft in the Pairs and Joyce Lindores, whom I had teamed up with to win the inaugural British Mixed Pairs Championship earlier in the year, was named as skip in the fours.

Joyce had Annette Evans from the Willow Bank Club in Glasgow at lead, Anne Watson from Loanhead Miners Welfare second and Janice Maxwell from Castle Douglas as third.

The venue for the bowls events was the four-green Pakuranga Club to the east of Auckland, and we set off for New Zealand on the 17th of January, arriving in Auckland after a horrendous fourty-one hour journey. Five days is hardly enough time for anyone to acclimatise to the change in conditions, and while it was bad enough for the bowlers, it must have been a lot worse for the athletes involved in the more physically demanding sports.

For the first time ever in the Commonwealth Games, the bowls events were not played in a complete round robin. Each event was divided into two sections with the sections made up on the basis of the finishing order in Edinburgh four years earlier, and there's no doubt we came off well in the deal.

We were included in Section 'B' with our main rivals looking to be New Zealand and Canada with Zambia, Papau New Guinea, Botswana, Cook Islands and newcomers India making up the Section.

The other group included World Champions Northern Ireland, England, Australia, Wales and Hong Kong — all potential medal winners. We had an added bonus as the two fours

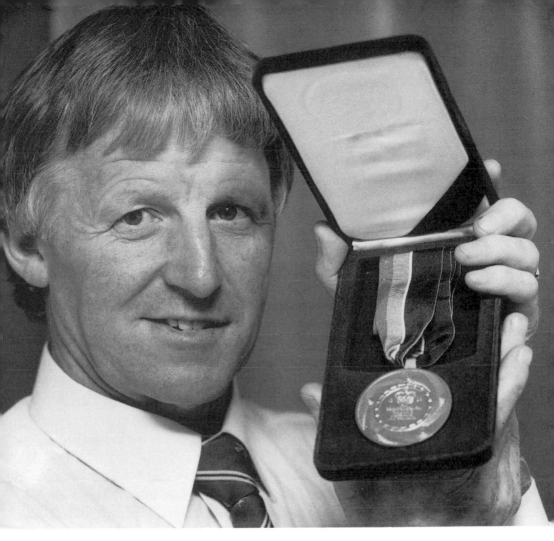

*I show my 1990 Commonwealth Games gold medal from Auckland.*

events, the men's and women's, were the last of the events to be decided — giving us an extra three days of practice.

The Pakuranga complex was very good, a lot better than the Henderson set-up that had hosted both the Men's and Women's World Championships in the previous two years, and the greens, all four of them, were good.

The Singles dominated the opening few days and Richard Corsie suffered a first-day setback. After a comfortable 25-13 win over Norfolk Island's Barry Wilson, Richard found himself punished on an outside rink, losing 25-12 to young Mark McMahon from Hong Kong. That put Dunfermline-born

McMahon in a strong position after an earlier 25-12 win over Port Talbot's John Price — another of the fancied medal contenders, and that was the way things worked out with McMahon powering his way through to the Gold Medal play-off with a seven out of seven record including a 25-17 win over defending champion Ian Dickison.

Corsie with wins over Botswana's Ray Mascarenhas 25-7, Western Samoa's Dick Hunt 25-8, Cook Islands' Philip Ulrich 25-6, and John Price 25-13, and a 25-20 defeat from Dickison won through to the Bronze Medal Play-off.

However, it was the other section that provided the real fireworks, with David Bryant, after a twelve-year absence, back in action and chasing a record fifth Singles Gold Medal. It looked odds on the old maestro would do just that when he coasted to six straight wins in his group matches, but amazingly Australia's Rob Parrella snatched a final spot in the last group match. Parrella, who had lost to David Corkill, needed to beat Bryant by at least 25-15 to go through to the final and after leading 23-7 he held off a late Bryant fightback for a 25-14 win and a final date with Mark McMahon.

That left Corsie and Bryant to fight it out for the Bronze Medal and despite heavy rain that wiped out half the day's play, Corsie continued his improved form with a 25-17 win. Parrella took the gold when he beat the twenty-year-old Hong Kong man 25-14 after surrendering a 7-0 lead as McMahon recovered to go 14-12 ahead after sixteen ends. Parrella, however, then produced a purple patch and reeled off the thirteen shots he needed for the Gold Medal over the next eight ends.

Our opening game in the fours was against newcomers India who had only arrived the day before the Games opened after a four-day period where their participation had been in doubt over visa problems. They did manage it, with their uniforms being delivered to the airport minutes before they left for Auckland, and they caused us some early problems, leading throughout the first ten ends. A count of seven, though, on the next put us 11-7 ahead and we pulled away to lead 18-8 after seventeen ends before a late rally from india left us 20-16 winners. We then took on Zambia later in the day and it was a similar story, trailing throughout the opening exchanges to leave Zambia 9-8 ahead after thirteen ends before we struck form and went on to win 22-10.

We had just one match the following day against Cook Islands, and this time there were no problems with a runaway 29-6 win and we then enjoyed a rest day with a three-out-of-three record. We resumed with a hard-fought 21-21 draw with Papua New Guinea, having to settle for a share of the spoils after holding a 19-15 lead with four ends to play, but all was forgiven when we edged home 18-17 against Phil Skoglund's New Zealand rink later in the day to put us on course for the final.

We had only Botswana and Canada to play and a dream start against Botswana quickly put the verdict in that one beyond doubt as we raced to a 15-2 lead after just eight ends, and we finally won 26-16. That left it a straight battle between ourselves and Papua New Guinea for a place in the final and as it turned out Papua lost 23-13 to Cook Islands in their final game — a result that put us in the final irrespective of what happened in our match with Bill Boettger's Canada side. We did win but not before Canada had made us work hard, leading 11-8 at twelve ends before we recovered to win 26-15.

So we were through to the final, and the opposition was Jim Baker's World Champions with Rod McCutcheon at lead, John McCloughlin second and Sammy Allen third. The Irish rink had snatched their final place when they took full advantage of a shock 21-14 defeat for Tony Allcock's England side from Hong Kong, beating Australia 17-14 to edge through a point clear of the Aussies and Hong Kong.

Before we met Northern Ireland in the last-day final, Scotland suffered a setback when we lost the Bronze Medal play off in the Women's Fours, surrendering a 14-2 seven end lead as Hong Kong recovered to snatch a 21-20 win. It really was the one that got away and it was the second time our women had lost out in the Bronze play-off with Sarah Gourlay and Frances Whyte going down 22-14 to England's Jayne Roylance and Mary Price in the Pairs.

In the other events, Senga McCrone finished third in her Women's Singles Section behind eventual Gold Medallist

Geua Tau from Papua New Guinea and Northern Ireland's Margaret Johnston, finishing with four wins from her seven matches. She came from 24-15 down to beat Zambia's Beatrice Mali 25-24, and added wins over Kay Dodd of Guernsey 25-10, Canada's Fatima Reimer 25-17 and Cook Island's Ngamarama Beniamina 25-11, but defeats from Tau 25-13, Johnston 25-20 and a 25-24 defeat from World Champion Janet Ackland of Wales left Senga out of the medals.

It was a similar story too for Graham Robertson and Angus Blair in the Men's Pairs, finishing with four wins and four defeats and in fourth place in their nine country section. They did score a 26-20 win over eventual Gold Medal winners Ian Schuback and Trevor Morris of Australia and they also beat England's Gary Smith and Andy Thomson 19-13, but they lost 29-20 to Northern Ireland's Victor Dallas and Ernie Parkinson and were edged out 18-14 in a great match by Kiwi's Rowan Brassey and Maurice Symes. They also went down 27-13 to Zimbabwe and threw away a 24-8 lead as Guernsey recovered to win 25-24. Their other wins came over Papau New Guinea 37-12 and Jersey 21-14.

We shared centre stage with the final of the Women's Fours between New Zealand and Australia on the last afternoon and there are no prizes for guessing which match held most interest for the spectators. It turned out to be a dissappointment for the home support with the Kiwis dropping two shots on the last end to lose 20-18, but just as the match finished we were in the middle of our final end but it didn't prevent them trooping noisily out of the surrounding stands, totally oblivious to our match. As I've said before, they can be rather parochial in New Zealand!

The opening exchanges were extremely tight and nervy with the first five ends confined to singles with us scoring on three of them. Northern Ireland broke the sequence with a double on the sixth end, but that was the only time they were in front. We regained the initiative with a double on the seventh end, and two successive counts of three pushed us 11-4 ahead.

Back came the Irish with Jim Baker in particular in great form and with seventeen ends played our lead had been

1974

1978

1982

1990

*I add my Commonwealth Games gold medal from the fours in New Zealand 1990, to my collection.*

trimmed to the minimum at 13-12. We picked up a double on the eighteenth but back came Ireland with a single to leave us 15-13 ahead with two to play.

Then Ian Bruce produced the shot that set up our gold medal win. With Ireland lying in good position I ask Ian to strike and he produced the perfect bowl, running the jack into the ditch and following through with his 'toucher' for shot, and when George and I added three more from our deliveries we picked up a four to lead 19-13 going into the last end.

A careless jack length left us in bother, as both Denis and Ian played a bad end, but we survived the crisis and kept Ireland to just a single for a 19-14 win and the Gold Medal.

So I had picked up where I had left off in Brisbane in 1982 and kept intact my record of picking up a medal in every Games I've played in, but, more importantly in my opinion, was that the top players were back in the Commonwealth Games fold. Had the International Bowling Board continued with their policy of 1986, then I'm sure the future of bowls in the Commonwealth Games woud have been in jeopardy.

If the top players are banned from competing, then the standard of play, and consequently the game, will suffer. That's why I think it was very important for the bowls events to include the Bryants, Allcocks and Woods of this World — not for any personal reasons, but for the good of bowls worldwide.

The fourteenth Games in New Zealand proved to be the most successful ever, thankfully free from the political boycotts that had overshadowed Edinburgh four years earlier and silenced the critics who had been predicting doom and gloom for the future of the Commonwealth Games.

Sportsmen, from whatever field, can look forward with confidence to Canada in 1994.

# CHAPTER FIFTEEN

## *The Future*

At fifty-two years of age the question I'm most often asked is how long I intend to continue playing top-level bowls. It really is the $64,000 question. I always answer that, God willing, I will play bowls as long as I can. When the time comes to bow out of the top level, I won't be locking the shoes and bowls away in some dark corner of the cupboard. I'll go back to club level and be quite happy to play away for as long as I can.

Having said that, I intend to be around at the top for a few years yet. I don't like tempting fate but I see no real reason why I can't continue for the next eight years anyway, which would take me to sixty. David Bryant, according to some pundits, has been on the decline for many years, yet he won the World Outdoor Championship at fifty-six and last year won the UK Indoor Championship a few days short of his fifty-eighth birthday — some decline!

Over the last two years I shed a lot of weight. The chunky Willie Wood has disappeared, not, I hasten to add, without a lot of hard work and a fairly strict watch on what I eat, and the stone and a half I've lost has certainly, in my opinion, helped my game.

In terms of ambition, obviously after two near misses in the World Outdoor Championships I would dearly love another shot at it. The next Championships are in Worthing in 1992, and while the Beach House Park greens have not been amongst my favourites, I can only hope that I'll still be playing well enough to be given another chance. That remains to be seen, and certainly there will be a lot more competition for the singles spot with players like Richard Corsie, Angus Blair, Hugh Duff and Graham Robertson all having claims.

Beach House Park has been the scene of two major disappointments when I went down twice in the final of the Woolwich Masters, and, on both occasions, to that man Bryant again.

The first came just a few months after my Auckland disappointment and when the final began, it really was a case of 'play it again Sam'.

On the opening end I drew two 'touchers'. David fired with his last bowl and, that's right, you've guessed it — he picked up a four. Conditions for the final were extremely difficult, with morning rain not having made things any easier and near gale-force winds adding to the problems.

After that dream start Bryant opened up an 8-0 lead and it was all uphill from that point on. Slowly, though, I got back into contention in what was a bit of a scrappy match, and with eighteen ends played it was anyone's match with David 19-17 ahead, but singles on the next two ends gave him a 21-17 win and the title for an incredible eighth time in eleven years.

The Masters on that occasion was staged on a straight knock-out format and I certainly didn't get things easy. In my first-round match with New Zealand's Rowan Brassey I had to finish with a burst of five shots over the last three ends to turn a sixteen-all scoreline into a 21-16 win, followed by a 21-14 quarter-final victory against Australia's Ian Schuback and a 21-17 semi-final win over Wynne Richards.

Twelve months later David and I were back in the final again, and this time conditions were a lot better and a capacity crowd turned out to see if I could avenge the previous year's defeat. The early rounds were played on a round-robin basis, with two sections of eight, although our group was reduced to seven before a bowl was delivered after World Championship Bronze Medallist Garin Beare of Zimbabwe withdrew after severe nose bleeding.

However, I qualified comfortably with wins over Kenny Williams (Australia), Tony Allcock (England), Cecil Bransky (Israel), John Bell (England), Robert Weale (Wales) and Rowan Brassey (New Zealand), a six-out-of-six record that left me three clear of second-placed Kenny Williams. David qualified from the other section with six wins — his sole defeat coming from fellow countryman, John Ottaway.

When the final began it turned into nothing short of a night-mare. Everything went wrong. David was brilliant. I couldn't do anything right, and before I knew what was happening I was 18-0 down. The games had been changed to twenty-five up in 1989, which was just as well, as a whitewash would have been looming had it been a twenty-one shot up match.

I did get off the mark and took my tally to eight before David clinched victory.

I've also played at Worthing in four international series and I can honestly say I've never been enamoured of the greens, and I know a lot of my international colleagues, including Tony All-cock, share my view. Let's hope the English Bowling Associa-tion and Worthing Council get their act together before 1992.

On the domestic front, a win in the Scottish Outdoor Singles is my dearest wish. I still often think back to my defeat from Dick Bernard in 1970. I would love to emulate my father's win of three years earlier, and of course a Scottish win in the next couple of years would strengthen my claim for the Singles spot in Worthing in 1992. I would also like to knock off one of the big Indoor titles, and being ranked in fourth place in the UK Ranking List at the start of 1989-90 season means that with reasonable performances I should be in the championships for the next couple of years.

On a more general note, the game is still enjoying a boom period, even allowing for the uncertainty that seems to sur-round some of the television events. Almost every couple of weeks there's some little eight-man tournament somewhere in the United Kingdom, and while the money may not be astron-omical it's usually not bad — around the £4,000 mark in total, with the winner normally pocketing something in the region of £1,500.

It's these sort of events that I feel could be the lifeblood of the international scene. The cost of staging the Home Interna-tionals as we know them today is escalating constantly, and it may be that the shorter invitation tournament will take over. I hope not — I think there's a place for both — but I do see a growth in the short, sharp, one or two day events.

Even in television terms, I'm not sure that the viewing public want the ten and eleven day events. I know from talking to David Harrison he is now of the opinion that perhaps the way ahead is to bring television in from the quarter-final stage for, say, the last four or five days.

I suppose it's inevitable when I contemplate the future that my mind goes back to some of the great characters I've known in the game, particularly during the early years. There just does not seem to be any characters about at present. I wonder how some of the old-time greats would have fared in the modern set up. Harry Reston, who sadly died towards the end of 1989, was perhaps the best known. Reston was incredible on the green, a real entertainer, but beneath all the showmanship was a brilliant player and a quite superb drawer of a shot. Harry won the Scottish Singles title in 1978 in his fiftieth year in bowls, beating one of my county colleagues, Jim Oliver from Macmerry, in the final. Harry was unquestionably born before his time: he would have been great for the modern-day television events.

At least one BBC producer, who shall remain nameless, thought so. At the 1972 World Championship at Worthing, *Grandstand* were taking in some of the action — an unuasual venture into the bowls world in these days — and Harry was in full flow. Out went the instructions to cameramen with the post-script — 'and let's have plenty of that noisy Scots bugger!'

Jock McAtee was another great who spanned three decades from his first international apearance in 1951. A railwayman from Catrine, he had a presence on the green that seemed to leave his opponents in awe. He notched up a record sixty-nine international appearances, a record I felt honoured to equal when I played at Worthing in 1989. McAtee was not only a superb player but a brilliant tactician, who thought about every aspect of the game.

He was a gentleman to play with or against and climaxed an incredible career when he won the Scottish Triples Championship at Queen's Park in 1985, when well into his seventies.

Another great player who, like McAtee, hailed from Ayrshire was Willie Moore, whose record probably should have been better that it was. Willie unfortunately carried much of his on-green enthusiasm into the post-match bar activities, and sadly much of his potential was never seen to its best advantage, but Willie was a great, great player.

Ireland had people like Gerry Crossey, Jim Donnelly and another Ayrshireman — Roy Fulton — who notched up an amazing seven wins in the Irish Singles Championship. Roy returned home a few years ago and continued his career at the Prestwick Indoor Club and showed advancing years had diminished little of his ability, winning the Prestwick Championship and then going all the way to the semi-finals of the Scottish Indoor Championship in 1986.

Wales had people like Jock Thomson and Jim Morgan and England players of the calibre of Robbie Stenhouse, Norman King and the like.

All of them, though, pale into insignificance beside David John Bryant CBE — quite simply the greatest bowler the world has ever known and ever will know. I have often been asked if I resent being about the bowls scene at the same time as David — as, unquestionably, he has cost me a lot of titles over the years. They couldn't be more wrong. Not only do I not resent it, I consider it a positive privilege to have played in the same era. I would like to think that when historians look back in future years they may well consider that had David Bryant not been about, Willie Wood would have won his share of World Titles. Players of the future won't experience what I consider the high-light of my bowling career — having been a contemporary of the greatest bowler the world has known — a man I look upon as a colleague, a rival and a great friend.

Another question that's often asked is whether I resent being in a sport that doesn't provide the big money that professionals in snooker, golf, tennis and the like enjoy. I would be less than honest if I didn't say there are times when, sitting in front of the television watching snooker players picking up six-figure first prizes, I think it would be nice to be playing for that sort of money, but, like everything in the world, there's a price to pay for it. Media exposure is obviously a lot greater, and not just in terms of reporting the snooker action.

The sickening levels some of the country's leading tabloid newspapers sink to in delving into people's private lives is nothing short of scandalous. Nothing, it appears, is sacred as they unravel some dark distant secret before a public with a seemingly insatiable appetite for scandal. Bowls so far has avoided that aspect of the media, and long may it continue.

There is also the added pressure that comes with the big money prizes. Snooker has its drug problems and beta blocker ban but it's a question that just doesn't arise in bowls. There is now random drug testing to comply with Sports Council regulations, but it's all treated by the players as a bit of a joke as we know that none of the top players would contemplate it.

I can also look back on the strides made in the game in the last decade. We have only been playing for prize money for the last eight years and everything takes time. Not that I think we will every reach the big league in terms of prize money and commercial spin-offs, but then in 1980 we didn't think we would have prize funds of £120,000 for the 1990 World Indoor Championships.

Who knows where it will all lead to?

I certainly don't, but I do know that if it were all to change tomorrow I would have no regrets. I've enjoyed every minute of it — even the disappointments. I've travelled the world playing the game I love. I've made countless friends and in recent years picked up a few bob along the way.

It's all a long way friom those early games back in Gifford with the half-crown reward from Colin Campbell. I wonder if my beneficiary ever imagined just how much effect his payments would have on the Gifford Bowling Club, Willie Wood, and the International Bowls World.

Here's to Worthing in 1992!

# Index

145

# Index

# Index

# Index

# Index